BUSINESS  E

Ronald Warson has wide experience of teaching business and commerce, including accounting and law. He has written textbooks on subjects ranging from business arithmetic and book-keeping to office practice and business organisation, and has served as Chief Examiner in Commerce, Structure of Business, Accounting and Business Mathematics for a number of bodies, including the RSA and AEB, and as a moderator for BTEC General courses.

TEACH YOURSELF BOOKS

BUSINESS AND COMMERCE

Ronald Warson

TEACH YOURSELF BOOKS

Hodder and Stoughton

First published 1984

British Library Cataloguing in Publication Data

Warson, Ronald
Business and commerce.—(Teach yourself books)
1. Commerce
I. Title
380.1   HF1009
ISBN 0 340 34310 9

Reproduced, printed and bound in Great Britain for
Hodder and Stoughton Educational,
a division of Hodder and Stoughton Ltd,
Mill Road, Dunton Green, Sevenoaks, Kent,
by Hazell Watson & Viney Limited,
Member of the BPCC Group,
Aylesbury, Bucks. Photoset by
Rowland Phototypesetting Ltd,
Bury St Edmunds, Suffolk.

Contents

Preface ix

1 General Survey of the Economic System 1
Introduction. Private enterprise. Central planning. Mixed economies. The structure and location of industry. Industry and commerce.

2 The Private Sector: Structure 11
The sole trader. The partnership. Joint-stock companies. The limited company. The internal organisation of a typical business.

3 The Private Sector: Finance 25
The Stock Exchange. A typical company and its finances.

4 The Public Sector; Co-operative Societies; Trade Unions 35

5 Retailing 46
The retail customer. Types of retail business. The changing pattern of retailing.

6 Wholesaling 60
The wholesale function. Bypassing the wholesaler. Types of wholesaler. The services of the wholesaler. Co-operative Wholesale Society. Wholesaling and industry. Wholesaling and agriculture. The future of the independent wholesaler.

7 Terms of Sale 67
A typical business transaction on credit. Value Added Tax.

8 Money and Banking 80
How and why banks began. Bills of exchange and credit.
The Bank of England and the money market.

9 The Commercial Banks 87
The functions of a commercial bank. Current accounts.
The clearing system. Credit transfer (bank giro) system.
Deposit accounts. What happens to money in the bank?
Borrowing from a bank. Other banking services.

10 The Post Office; British Telecom 106
The Post Office. Communications services of the Post
Office. Postal services. British Telecommunications. Future development.

11 Accounting Principles 116
The capital of a business. Effect of transactions on a
balance sheet. Interpretation of a simple balance sheet.
Loan capital. Turnover: profits and losses. Calculation of
profit.

12 Transport 128
The background. The railways since 1945. Concept of
unit load – containers. Developments in shipping. Civil
aviation. Pipelines. Problems of road and rail transport.

13 Insurance 142
Uninsurable risks. History of insurance. Principles of
insurance. Organisation of British insurance. Reinsurance. British insurance overseas. The insurance
ombudsman. The main types of insurance policies. Insurance money and influence.

14 Overseas Trade 157
The advantages of foreign trade. The pattern of world
trade. The terms of trade. International financial institutions. Balance of trade and balance of payments. Conduct of the export trade. Conduct of the import trade.
Abolition of exchange control. Britain and the European
Economic Community.

15 Central and Local Government 176
Central government. Local government.

16 Consumer Protection   182
     Common law. Statute law. Encouraging competition.

Commercial Abbreviations   190
Glossary of Commercial Terms   194
Sources of Information   206
Examination Questions   207
Multiple-Choice Test   215
Answers to multiple-choice test   224
Index   225

Preface

Business and Commerce is, because of its particular relevance to modern life, becoming of greater interest to the general reader, and is being studied, for various examinations, by increasing numbers of students. The main purpose of this book is to present in a readable manner a balanced picture of the business world. The author would not be honest if he claimed that this book and this book alone provides the reader with a very detailed knowledge of specific areas of business (e.g. banking, insurance): obviously more specialist texts need to be consulted for this purpose. But it does provide a broad general knowledge of the whole field of business. It illustrates the general nature and purpose of commercial activities in the UK, the functions of the main business institutions and their interlocking relationships. Its aim is to give the reader, whether a student or not, the feel of commercial life.

The text begins with a short survey of the UK economic system and then proceeds to deal with the different forms of business organisation in both the private and the public sectors. All aspects of trade, and the ancillary services that make trade possible, are covered in subsequent chapters (including marketing, banking, insurance, consumer protection, communications, transport, overseas trade); the inter-relationships of these branches of commerce are clearly explained, as are those activities of central and local government that affect the life of the business community. A comprehensive list of commercial abbreviations and a glossary of commercial terms are also provided.

Particular care has been taken to ensure that the book is especially useful for the student. As well as being a basic introductory book for GCE Ordinary level, it is eminently suitable for those taking Elements of Commerce (London Chamber of Commerce) and should prove valuable to Royal Society of Arts examinees in the Background to Business papers (Stages I and II). Business and Technician Education Council (BTEC) students will find that the Business and Commerce parts of the World of Work module (General level) are more than adequately covered by this text. Furthermore, it is strongly recommended for students beginning a course in Economics or the GCE Advanced level in Business Studies – it will make valuable preliminary reading for them, as it will for all BTEC National level students.

A word of warning. Because of the rapid pace of economic and technical change in our advanced industrial society, it is vital that the reader attempts to keep his commercial knowledge up to date – selective reading of the business pages of newspapers combined with selective listening to, or viewing of, appropriate radio and television programmes will help enormously. In addition, various commercial institutions and public authorities issue readable and informative booklets on a wide range of subjects, and some of these are listed at the end of the book.

I express sincere thanks to the staff of the publishers for their very considerable help to me in the preparation of this book; any errors are, however, my responsibility.

Ronald Warson

1

General Survey of the Economic System

Introduction

Air is abundant. Unless we are deep-sea divers or space explorers there is more than enough of it to satisfy all our needs, wherever we may be on the world's surface. This is not true, however, of all the other goods that we require to preserve and enrich life. People must make decisions and be prepared to work in order to grow food, manufacture cloth and build roads; in these processes natural wealth such as iron ore and fertile soil is used up; machinery wears out and has to be replaced. Economic resources, in short, must be used, and since only a limited quantity can be pressed into service over any period of time, there is considerable scope for arguing over what shall be produced. But not only goods are necessary to satisfy people's needs. A bus ride or a doctor's attention may in certain circumstances be just as important as a loaf of bread, and services such as these also use up resources. Furthermore, machine tools, lorry space, and many other goods and services that are of no direct value to the ordinary person must be created in order that the supply of consumer goods like food and household goods can be kept up and increased.

In the United Kingdom, as in other advanced industrial societies, the network of decision-taking, of production and distribution is very complex and sophisticated, but this highly developed complexity makes it possible for us to enjoy a standard of living superior to that of most of the world's peoples, who live in simpler societies.

The subject of economics is concerned with the whys and wherefores of production and distribution. In this book we are not primarily concerned with these matters but more with the economic structure that exists in modern states, particularly the United Kingdom, and especially with those topics that deal with the exchange of goods and services. Some elementary, basic knowledge of economics is necessary to assist the student to a fuller understanding of business and commerce.

Private enterprise

Private enterprise is one of the systems under which a country's economic activities can be organised. Perhaps organised is the wrong word, for the essence of private enterprise is that each individual manages his economic life in whichever way he thinks fit. Anyone is free to become a businessman and to enter any field of production he likes, or to offer his labour and skills to an employer. The man with money may lend it as profitably as he can, and the owner of land can rent it out without hindrance. In theory, this should result in the best of all possible worlds. The manufacturer, for example, eager to outdo his rivals, lowers his prices so as to persuade people to buy from him, while at the same time he puts up wages so that men will prefer to work for him.

In such a private-enterprise system, price is the pivotal mechanism by which it is decided what shall be produced. If consumers' demand for a particular product rises, the price of it rises and the manufacturers make extra profits. New producers, encouraged by the high profits, enter the industry, and the quantity of the product put on the market increases. This extra supply causes the price to fall again. Alternatively, should demand for a product fall, the price falls, and this brings financial difficulties to those firms that were just managing to make ends meet at the old price. The supply of the goods contracts, and so the price rises. The requirements of the industries producing consumer goods influence the types of machinery and other producers' goods that will be turned out. It is clear that, in the final analysis, the wishes of the consumers of goods and services decide the composition of output in a private-enterprise economy. The consumers are, of course, nothing more than the population of a country in the role of spenders of money.

There might seem to be many incontestable advantages in such a system, and so it appeared to the early economists of the eighteenth century who advocated the removal of government regulation from the economic life of Britain. History, however, rapidly showed that private enterprise had severe drawbacks and was most unlikely to function in the best interests of all. In general, manufacturers dislike competing and tend to combine, especially in those fields of production where large-scale working brings economies. Monopolies can arise, capable of charging the public prices that yield the highest profits and exhibiting a take-it-or-leave-it attitude to people seeking employment. The price system will cause those goods to be produced that people can afford, rather than those that they really ought to have. Thus, in a society with a very unequal distribution of income, some persons may, through poverty, be denied health services and education, while others squander the country's resources on items many might consider to be luxuries.

The widespread social distress in the early nineteenth century in Britain, within an economic framework of almost total private enterprise, convinced many that private enterprise was irretrievably bad and should be replaced by a system of state control. This idea first became a reality when the Soviet Union was created after the Russian revolution of 1917.

Central planning

In central planning the government determines in advance what shall be produced. To ensure that its decisions are carried out it normally owns the means of production and distribution within its borders. Thus a rigidly controlled output is substituted for the constantly changing variety of goods and services turned out in a private-enterprise economy. It is usual for the planning authority to plan the composition of the nation's output over periods of five or more years. Such a system has its advantages for a poor country bent on rapid development: planning can channel the country's resources away from the manufacture of luxury goods (which, while satisfying the immediate wants of some, do nothing to promote the future well-being of the nation as a whole) into the creation of roads, irrigation improvements and steel mills, which may eventually mean increasing standards of living for all.

Central planning, however, has its drawbacks. Planners may

make mistakes, may be politically motivated and may sometimes be corrupt. Too fervent an ambition to develop a country in a short period of time can cause such a large proportion of the resources available to be diverted to the creation of producers' goods that the standard of living of the people may be unduly depressed. Furthermore, when each individual is required to live his life in accordance with a long-term economic plan, he is bound to lose a considerable degree of economic freedom, and many societies find this idea intolerable.

In a centrally planned economy, the price system could, in theory, be abolished. The government, having decided what variety of consumer goods needs to be produced, distributes them to the people in line with some predetermined set of rules. In practice, gross inefficiencies in the use of economic resources are likely to result, and so it is normal for people to receive wages and buy goods in shops as in a private-enterprise system. However, price in this context is essentially just a smooth mechanism for distributing goods and services to consumers. Excess demand for one item does not bring about an increase in supply, and if the high demand seems likely to continue rationing will be introduced. Propaganda can be used to divert interest away from goods that the government wishes to keep in short supply, and many varieties of products familiar in private-enterprise societies may just not appear in the shops.

Mixed economies

Most countries have 'mixed' economies: private enterprise and government sectors exist side by side. This is so in the United Kingdom, where an increasing degree of government intervention has been accepted in a basically private-enterprise system. By means of Acts of Parliament, government agencies, ministries, and the massive effects of taxation and departmental expenditure, the government has extended its influence and control into all spheres of economic life.

Large areas of industry – coal mining, electricity generation, the railways – are openly state-owned, and in many other instances – for example, some provincial bus undertakings – government control is no less real for being less obvious. Local authorities, too, add to the volume of enterprises in official ownership by running local transport services, airports and street markets.

However, a Conservative government elected in 1979 pledged to drastically reduce state control of public services, and a number of nationalised undertakings were 'privatised'. The reader will find more about this in Chapter 4.

Private enterprise still accounts for a large proportion of the output of goods and services in the United Kingdom, but even here state influence is considerable. Computers, aircraft construction and other great industries that, by their output, pricing, export and employment policies, have important effects on the economy as a whole, receive much supervision and assistance. Laws exist which may be used to restrain firms from combining into monopolies, and to prevent or restrict manufacturers' control over the prices charged for their products by retailers. Taxation policies can be used to influence the sales of various types of goods, to stimulate exports and to influence the managers of new or expanding firms in their choice of suitable places for setting up their plant. Sometimes the government will make direct grants to private industry, as it has done regularly in shipbuilding and civil aviation, and as it did in furtherance of a particular policy when the textile and computer industries were reorganised in the early 1960s and 1970s.

Health, education and the social services, though not generally thought of as industries, are largely under centralised control, thereby ensuring, as in a centrally planned economy, that the allocation of the benefits involved is made on a basis of need rather than wealth.

Finally, the supply of money in the economy, obtained by the public mainly from their local bank branches but also from other financial institutions, comes originally from the Bank of England, a publicly owned institution.

The structure and location of industry

In a mixed economy system goods and services are produced by industries, large and small, some of which, as we have seen, are state-owned and some of which are privately owned. In most instances, industries are divided up into a number of firms; in other cases, the total production of a commodity is monopolised by one firm. Nationalised industries are, generally, monopolies or near monopolies since, although prior to state control they may have consisted of many firms, government ownership combines these firms into a single unit. However, in some instances some private competition has been introduced: for example British Caledonian (a public limited company) competes on a number of scheduled routes with the state-owned British Airways.

Large firms producing large outputs often have advantages over small firms. Employees can become specialised in various parts of the production process, so avoiding the waste of time when a man moves from one job to another, or the loss of efficiency when he tackles a job to which he is not suited. Since it will be used constantly, it becomes worthwhile to install specialised equipment. A large firm can buy its supplies of raw materials and components in bulk, which is usually cheaper, and economise on marketing by selling in large quantities. All these, and other, advantages reduce the cost to a firm of each unit of output, so enabling it to put its product on the market at a lower price than its smaller-scale rivals must charge. It is not surprising, therefore, that the most successful industries in the United Kingdom are those where the constituent firms are able to make use of economical large-scale production methods. Thus we have the spectacular expansion of the motor and chemical industries since the last war. Economists refer to these advantages as *economies of scale*. However, it must be realised that in certain circumstances *diseconomies of scale* arise (i.e. unit costs may rise). For example, a stage may be reached when efficient management becomes difficult because a business has become too large to control properly.

Large-scale operation is not appropriate to all industries. Retailing must, by its very nature, in many of its areas be fragmented into small units in order to reach the market and provide the service the customers require. A considerable degree of large-scale working has become possible where one firm owns a series of branch shops, but up to now this has only been successful in certain categories of goods in particular market situations. Despite technological improvements, retailing is still a comparatively labour-intensive industry.

Of course, just because an industry consists of large firms, it does not automatically mean that it will be prosperous. If the market for the product is declining, specialised equipment and elaborate organisation in a firm can be a liability, since it has to be serviced and paid for, but may not be sufficiently well used to pay its way. The coal industry in Britain, for example, faces difficulties because of the competition from alternative fuels like oil and liquid gas, which in some circumstances may be more efficient. Coal production has been reduced considerably in the last twenty years, though as a result of the artificial oil crises created by some producing countries in 1973 the closures of pits (unless exhausted) has been drastically slowed down in recent years.

The contraction of industries such as coal brought social problems in its wake, of which the most serious was unemployment. Many regions of the country that became highly developed in the nineteenth century relied on a few basic industries which have lost their importance this century. South Wales relied on coal and steel, South Lancashire on textiles, and Northumberland and Durham on coal, steel and shipbuilding. Steel has remained a vital material, but as coal output, textile manufacture and ship construction have declined, people have been put out of work. The great efforts made by successive governments in the last forty years to deal with the problems that arose from the running down of these heavy industries were an important example of government willingness to intervene in the country's economic life. Large portions of the United Kingdom have been designated areas for expansion, and incentives in the form of tax reliefs and grants are given to firms willing to set up or expand in these areas. The development areas concerned extend over large tracts of country and do not just cover districts of high unemployment. This is to ensure that firms are not restricted too narrowly in their choice of location, and also that the more sparsely populated areas of Britain are brought into the general scheme of national development.

However, a general world trade recession in the late 1970s, coupled with the coming to power of a government in the UK pledged to 'let market forces prevail', led to vast increases in unemployment. In general, since 1979 government financial assistance to industry has declined in real terms.

Industry and commerce

The reader will have noticed that the word 'industry' has been used to refer not only to the production of goods but also to the production of services. People tend to make a rigid distinction between activities that involve obtaining and changing the form of resources and goods, and activities that change the position of goods in place or time, labelling the one productive and the other unproductive. They consider that the term industry refers more correctly to the first group, which covers mining, agriculture and manufacture. In economics such a distinction is meaningless: the driver who transports a radio set from the factory to a shop, the typist who produces the invoices recording the sale and the retailer who keeps the set on his premises until a customer wishes to buy it are helping as much towards the satisfaction of a need as the factory employee who assembles the radio set.

Classification of productive occupations

All occupations can be divided into four main productive branches: the first two can be described as industrial, and the third and fourth comprise two groups of services.

1 *Primary or extractive occupations.* All types of agriculture, mining and fishing. These are, of course, the basic occupations that man has carried on for thousands of years.
2 *Manufacturing and constructive occupations.* Persons in this broad group convert the raw materials provided by those in group 1 into a great variety of products: examples are steel (heavy industry), TV sets (light industry). The construction trades (building and civil engineering) are in this category.
3 *Commercial service occupations.* Those in these occupations are concerned directly or indirectly with the movement of goods from the producer to the consumer or user, that is, they are connected with distribution in its broadest sense. The reader will see from the remainder of this chapter the relationship between the different commercial occupations.
4 *Direct service occupations.* These services are usually of a personal nature and are not connected with commerce. Examples are teachers, doctors, police, various public officials, entertainers.

The more developed an economy becomes, the more the weight of employment moves towards groups 3 and 4. At present, in the United Kingdom, about the same proportion of the labour force is employed in commercial and direct services combined as in manufacturing and construction; the number of people employed in agriculture is less than 4% of the total labour force, whereas before 1780 it was over 80%. It is only the countries with high standards of living that can afford to employ large numbers of persons in direct services (in the UK about one quarter of the working population is so engaged), since the basic requirements of these people have to be met by the remainder employed in production and distribution.

Commercial activities, then, are one of the necessary sets of activities that contribute towards meeting the economic needs of the community. It is usual to divide commerce into six branches: trade, storage, banking, insurance, communications and transport, all of which are concerned with, or ancillary to, the distribution of goods. It should be remembered that buyers of goods are not only householders obtaining their domestic needs: commerce also comes into play in getting raw materials to processing works and components to assembling plants.

Trade covers the actual marketing of goods. Raw materials are often subjected to a wide variety of processes and pass through many hands before they reach the final consumer. Much expert knowledge comes into play in ensuring smooth and efficient buying and selling between factory manager, wholesaler, retailer and shopper. Many specialists are employed in the business of 'trade' – for example, buyers, market research and advertising experts.

Closely connected with trade is storage or warehousing. Expensive facilities are provided, and money must be tied up at various successive points in the process of production and distribution so that stocks of goods can be held for varying periods of time. This becomes necessary when goods are awaiting shipment, or when demand temporarily falls off; goods are also commonly held in stock in order to meet, without delay, a sudden unexpected increase in demand.

One of the principal functions of banks is to provide the economy with the money it requires to maintain its operations smoothly. In addition, banks provide a variety of services of use to the businessman – facilities to borrow money, expert advice, the provision of foreign currency and so forth.

Insurance allows risks to be taken without fear of loss. A firm may, by paying relatively small regular amounts of money to an insurance company, be certain of being compensated if it suffers financially through calamities such as fire or burglary. There is no doubt that insurance, by providing this sort of protection, encourages much economic enterprise that otherwise would not be undertaken.

Transport facilities are made use of in order to move goods physically. A good transport system is a hallmark of a developed country, and all developing countries set a high priority on the construction of roads and railways, docks and airports.

It is the study of business and commerce, then, that this book deals with – all aspects of trade and the auxiliary services that make trade possible; of the business units that control and provide these ancillary services; and of the government agencies that assist business and the community generally.

2

The Private Sector: Structure

In dividing business concerns into different categories we are not so much concerned with the type of business (e.g. retailer, wholesaler) as with its form or structure. This and the next chapter are going to consider the different types of businesses that exist, look at the distinguishing features of each category, and consider both advantages and disadvantages. The reader should realise that there is no standard pattern of organisation; rather the position is that different types have evolved to meet the changing demands of our social and economic systems.

The most important, but not the only, factor influencing the form of organisation is the amount of capital (or resources) needed. Thus it is obvious that, whereas a small retail shop can probably be owned by one person who has provided the resources required from his own savings or borrowings, this type of business unit would scarcely be satisfactory for car manufacturing. In Chapter 1 it was shown how the UK economy was divided basically into the private and the public sectors; both these will be considered in some detail, and co-operative societies with their rather special characteristics will also be dealt with. In Chapter 4, p.42, a table is given summarising the main features of each type of business unit.

Basically, any unit in the private sector exists for the purposes of private profit. It may have one owner (sole trader); or two or more owners up to a normal limit of twenty (partnership); or it may have company or corporate status (e.g. a limited liability company). Each of these types will now be considered in turn.

The sole trader

This is the oldest form of business unit and even today forms the largest group in numbers, though not in importance. It is a common mistake to assume that nearly all sole traders are retailers of goods; certainly there is a very large number of sole traders in this field, but it must be remembered that there are many other types of businesses in the one-man owner category, for example farmers and the business professions (solicitors, estate agents, doctors, etc.), as well as many small service businesses (garages, jobbing builders, hairdressers, etc.).

One person is responsible for providing the capital (either from his own resources or possibly by borrowing) and for managing the business; and, of course, this person takes all the risks of the enterprise. No legal formality is needed before this type of business can come into being (though, of course, there may well be licensing and byelaw requirements to fulfil in certain trades).

The main disadvantages of this type of business unit are that it may be difficult to expand owing to shortage of capital and that the owner may not possess the necessary qualifications enabling him to handle all sides of the business – thus he may not be competent to deal with, say, display or accountancy work. Furthermore, the sole proprietor has to take unlimited liability for his business debts – that is, in the event of the business running into financial difficulties, he will have to use his private funds (and sell private possessions and property as well if necessary) to make good any deficiency. This is because a sole trader is not recognised as a separate legal being or entity; thus the 'The Corner Stores' owned by Alexander Young is merely Alexander Young trading under a business name. The Registration of Business Names Act 1916, which required any business operating under a name other than the true name of its owner(s) to register with the Department of Trade, has been repealed. However, the 1981 Companies Act requires *any* business (sole trader, partnership or registered company) which is carried on under a name other than that of its owner, to display particulars of its ownership on its business premises and business stationery. In addition, these particulars must be supplied in writing, on request, to any customers or suppliers. Local authority trading standards officers (see page 181) have a duty to enforce these provisions of the Act.

The partnership

To avoid some of the disadvantages mentioned above a partnership may be formed. This is merely an association of two or more persons 'carrying on a business in common with a view to profit' (Partnership Act 1890). The last five words of the definition have the effect, of course, of excluding non-profit-making organisations like youth and sports clubs. The maximum number of partners allowed is twenty, though certain professional partnerships may now exceed this figure (solicitors, accountants, stockbrokers); furthermore, it is possible that in the future the Department of Trade and Industry may use the power to allow other types of business to exceed the limit of twenty. The principle of unlimited liability again arises – in fact, it is possible that in the event of financial difficulty a partner may have to make a greater contribution from private funds than the sum proportionately required by his capital, simply because another partner cannot meet his proper share of the deficiency owing to insufficient private funds. Thus if originally A had invested £30000 and B £15000, and owing to unsuccessful trading there was a deficiency of £9900, then if A had private means of £10000 and B only £2000, A would be compelled to contribute £7900 to meet the deficiency (i.e. almost four times as much as B).

There is no legal obligation for partners to enter into a formal agreement. If they do not do so, then the partnership relies on the provisions of the 1890 Act. These are principally that all partners share profits and losses equally; have a right to participate in management; and must agree before new partners can be admitted. If, however, a formal Partnership Agreement or Deed is drawn up, then the agreed provisions override those in the Partnership Act. Typical information likely to be included in an agreement includes:

1 The amount of capital to be contributed by each partner.
2 The way in which profits and losses are to be shared.
3 The management responsibilities of each partner.
4 The maximum drawings of cash for personal use by each partner.
5 The provisions both for the introduction of new partners and for the dissolution of the partnership.

Remember that the partners may not necessarily divide profits in the same ratio as their capital contributions. It may well be arranged that a partner may be allowed a greater share of profits because of an additional contribution he makes to the business; thus he may possess certain skills or may have personal contacts which will lead to extra income for the partnership. Again, one partner may work full-time, whereas another may well be part-time only, or even be a non-working (i.e. sleeping) partner; often the working partner will be compensated by being allowed a fixed 'salary' before the division of profits.

So that a partner with limited liability only can be admitted to a business, the Limited Partnership Act of 1907 was passed. Such a partner (called a limited partner) cannot be required to use private funds in the event of financial difficulties. However, he cannot participate in management at all, and therefore it will be seen that there must be at least one ordinary partner in a partnership (i.e. taking unlimited liability). In point of fact, few limited partnerships have been registered since the Act was passed – altogether there have been rather less than 2000 over the intervening period, and since 1960 there have been some hundreds only. It is generally more satisfactory to form a limited company if limited liability is required (see page 15).

A difficulty can often arise as a result of the sudden death of a member of a partnership. Although the business may be in a sound position, it may not have sufficient cash available to pay out to the estate of the deceased person. A solution is for the business to take out a Partnership Survivorship Assurance (see page 155), which will ensure that sufficient funds are available.

Partnerships may be found in a wide range of businesses. Retailers and wholesalers commonly adopt this form of undertaking, and it is also quite common in fairly small-scale manufacturing businesses. Many professional firms (e.g. solicitors, architects, doctors) are organised as partnerships; they are also suitable for temporary enterprises since the agreement can easily contain provisions for terminating the partnership by notice. It is also true that a partnership *may* have a lower tax liability than that of a limited company, but the tax structure is a highly complicated one and it is dangerous to generalise.

Finally, it is important to mention that, irrespective of whether there is a formal legal agreement or not, it is essential that partners act with complete integrity towards their colleagues and have confidence in each other, otherwise a business may well be jeopardised. Each partner commits the firm in the *ordinary* course of business, and in return he is indemnified by the firm against any loss he may suffer whilst so acting.

Joint-stock companies

So far, two types of business unit have been looked at, the sole trader and the partnership, and it was seen that a basic similarity of both is that the law merely treats them as one or several persons trading either individually or as a group – neither is a separate legal entity. Now a category of unit – the joint-stock company – will be discussed. This is in law an artificial 'person'; that is, it has 'life' of its own apart from that of its members; it is an 'incorporated' body. It can contract in its own name, can sue and be sued, and does not 'die' until legally dissolved, even though its individual members may change from time to time (whether through death, retirement or mere unwillingness to remain members).

Companies have existed in the United Kingdom for many hundreds of years: they were first important in Tudor times in the field of foreign trade. Many of the earliest companies were created by Royal Charter, such as the Hudson's Bay Company 1672, and later companies were created by individual Acts of Parliament (examples were the railway, gas and electricity undertakings – all now 'nationalised', see Chapter 4). Nowadays, the Royal Charter method is not used for trading companies but can still be utilised for the creation of professional bodies (e.g. Institute of Chartered Secretaries and Administrators). Although some companies created by individual Acts still exist (some water-supply companies, for example), this is obviously an expensive and impractical way to form a company. It is the Act of Parliament creating the statutory company that lays down its powers and limits the financial liability of its members in some manner.

By the middle of the nineteenth century it was necessary to have some general method of creating trading companies. The factory system had come into being, and this necessitated the raising of large sums of capital to finance mass-production methods. The partnership was not satisfactory for this purpose because of the unlimited liability principle (though it was possible to limit this liability to some extent and under certain circumstances); further-more, some method was needed whereby under a legislative umbrella those wishing to raise capital and those wanting to invest should be brought together. The 1844 Companies Act set out a system of registration of companies, but it was the 1855 Act that provided generally for the first time that limited liability could be granted to investors. Subsequent Acts amended and extended the regulations, and company law is now basically stated in a series of Companies Acts (1948–1981). In general, it can be said that the whole purpose of these Acts is to provide safeguards for those who have invested (shareholders); those who intend to invest; those who are owed money by companies (creditors); or those who may be considering contracting with companies – while at the same time laying down procedures to enable companies to be created, to expand, to change their form, and to dissolve.

Until 1980 there were three types of company that could be registered, but now there are only two:

1 Companies limited by shares

These are the vast majority, and all commercial trading businesses that become incorporated fall into this category. There are over three quarters of a million in this group, which can be subdivided into *public* companies and *private* companies. In the former case, the general public may be invited to become members and the transfer of shares is normally effected through a stock exchange – see Chapter 3. A private company, however, may not have a public offer of shares, and until the 1980 Companies Act became law had to restrict the right to transfer its shares – usually by giving the directors discretion whether or not to register a transfer – and to limit the number of its members to fifty, not counting employee shareholders.

Now these two provisions have been repealed, provided a private company amends its rules (see *Articles of Association*, page 19), it can have the prospect of growth and development hitherto open only to the public company. However, because it is still illegal for a private company to have a public issue of shares, there is obviously a limit, in general, to the extent of such growth and development that will be possible.

But there may well be an opportunity for non-public share offers on a localised basis by private companies. At present there are about 10 000 public companies and around 750 000 private companies, the great majority of the latter in the small- or medium-size range. Public limited companies must include these three words in their title, though the abbreviation Plc is legally acceptable and in general use. Private companies continue to employ the word 'limited', as for example ABC Limited or ABC Ltd.

Generally, it is much simpler legally, and very much cheaper, to form a private company than a public company. Both now require a minimum of two members, but a public company must have an authorised and issued capital of at least £50 000 (see page 40).

The 1981 Companies Act has, as its prime purpose, the harmonisation of company law in the European Economic Community (EEC). Additionally, the Act introduced detailed rules on the format of the published accounts: previously, though all companies had to disclose certain information, the way the accounts were drawn up was at the discretion of the companies themselves.

2 Unlimited companies

These have the advantage of incorporation, but liability of individual members (as with partnerships) is unlimited. Not unnaturally these companies are uncommon, but because the 1967 Companies Act provided that all limited companies must publish their accounts (until then the majority of private limited companies did not have to do so) there have been a number of cases where limited companies have become unlimited ones to avoid having to do this. The best-known example is that of the C & A Modes group of department stores. It is doubtful whether large numbers of limited companies will choose the same course. Under the 1980 Act an unlimited company can now only be a private company.

Companies limited by guarantee

Here the founder members (or an executive committee) agree to be liable for debts up to a fixed limit (often £1). This is merely a device to secure the benefits of incorporation and limited liability for non-trading, non-profit-making organisations that do not have shareholders. The majority of the professional associations (e.g. the Institute of Freight Forwarders) come within this group, and sports and social clubs also often become companies limited by guarantee. There have been about 300 to 500 registrations yearly in this category. However, the 1980 Act forbade the future formation of such companies.

The limited company – its main features

Persons wishing to form a company must submit certain documents to the Registrar of Companies (Department of Trade).

The two most important ones, which are dealt with below, are the Memorandum of Association and the Articles of Association. The Certificate of Incorporation which is issued enables a private company to commence business. A public company may not do so until it receives a Certificate of Trading, and to qualify for this the company must have allotted (i.e. issued) shares up to a certain minimum subscription; this is to ensure that the company will have sufficient capital to enable it to commence trading.

It must be mentioned at this stage that, in practice, a public limited company must satisfy further stringent requirements laid down by the Council of the Stock Exchange (see Chapter 3).

The Memorandum of Association

This provides the world at large with certain basic information about the company. It contains:

1 *The Name Clause.* Subject to the approval of the Department of Trade, a company may choose any name it likes. The Department will not agree to any name being used that too closely resembles that of another company, particularly in the same type of business; neither will it sanction names containing words that suggest it has connections with some official body (e.g. The Borough of Greenwich Domestic Stores Ltd). 'Limited' must be a part of the name, though non-trading bodies like charities and professional associations may be given permission to drop the use of the word (such as British Red Cross). If a company wishes to trade under a name other than its registered one, then it must also conform to the 1981 Act requirement referred to on page

12. The European Communities Act now makes it necessary to include the registered number of the company and its registered address on business documents.

2 *The Registered Office.* It is necessary to state whether this is to be in England and Wales or in Scotland, as the latter has a different set of laws.

3 *The Objects Clause.* In order that persons investing capital will know in advance that this is only to be used for specific purposes, a company must register its objects, that is, the type of business it intends to undertake. To avoid the necessity of having to amend these objects if the company subsequently decides to trade in another field, it is usual to state these in as wide a way as possible (e.g. 'general retailing' rather than 'retailing of grocery'). Acting outside its powers, *ultra vires*, is illegal, and agreements would be void. The Courts interpret objects clauses in a flexible way to cover necessary ancillary activities (e.g. a department store could obviously run its own training school for employees).

4 *The Limitation Clause.* This shows whether the company is limited by shares or guarantee.

5 *Capital Clause.* This gives details of the proposed amount of share capital and the different categories of shares.

6 *Association Clause.* The names of the founder members (minimum seven if a public company) and the number of shares each has subscribed for are included.

Articles of Association
These are the rules governing the internal affairs of a company – for example, voting rights of the different categories of shareholders, conduct of general meetings of shareholders, election of directors, and so on. Companies may either accept the set of model rules contained in the Companies Acts or accept them subject to certain amendments, or they may draw up their own special articles. A company can alter its articles by special resolution, and a private company can, subject to certain provisions, convert into a public limited company; though this is only likely where a flourishing private company wishes to expand and needs an injection of a considerable amount of capital.

Types of capital

Nominal (or authorised registered) capital. This is the total amount of capital the company *may* raise.

Issued capital. The proportion of the nominal capital that has actually been issued. In practice, because getting authority to increase nominal capital is complicated, though possible, it is usual to register a higher nominal capital than is likely to be needed. Capital may be in any convenient unit (25p, 50p, £1); the size of the unit has no significance – £1 is the most common. Furthermore, a company may not wish the shareholders to pay the full value of the shares when they are applied for. A £1 share could be issued on the following terms: 25p in the £ when the shares are applied for; 50p when they are issued or allotted; and 25p six months later. Nowadays, however, companies normally ask for the full amount to be paid on application. Once shares have been fully paid there can be no further financial liability on shareholders; in the example given above there is a liability until the shares are fully paid for.

Types of shares

Preference shares. Owners of this type of share receive their dividends (share of profits) before other shareholders and normally receive repayment of capital first in the event of dissolution. Most preference shares are cumulative ones; this means that if, owing to lack of profits, a dividend has not been paid in any year, then these arrears must be made up before other shareholders receive any payments. Preference shares carry a fixed dividend rate; for example, the holder of £100 7% preference stock would receive £7 per annum. Preference shares appeal to institutional buyers such as banks, insurance companies, the Church, trade unions, pension funds, who want a steady and comparatively safe income. Some preference shares are redeemable (see below).

Ordinary shares. The majority (or often all) of the capital of a company consists of this type of share. It does not carry a fixed rate of dividend and the shareholder only receives dividend payment after the preference shareholders are satisfied. In a good trading year the percentage dividend paid to these ordinary shareholders is likely to be much higher than that paid to preference shareholders.

An example of the capital structure of a fictitious company showing dividend calculation is given in the following chapter.

Until 1981 a company could not normally 'purchase' its own shares and could only 'redeem' (i.e. buy back) redeemable preference shares. Now a company can issue redeemable shares of any category – preference, ordinary and so on – provided it also has in issue non-redeemable shares. This prevents a company redeeming all its shares and finishing up without shareholders. Additionally a company can purchase its own shares, again provided that after the purchase there remain some non-redeemable shares in issue – for a company must have, at all times, at least two members.

In general, the overall effects of the 1980 and 1981 Acts have been to reduce restrictions on smaller businesses whilst introducing new rules on a number of issues where previously there had been some public anxiety; for example, extending the law requiring disclosure of interest in a company's shares. Public companies are the category affected by these rules.

The internal organisation of a typical business

Any well-managed organisation, even if it is small and informal, must operate within a framework. This includes arrangement of staffing and allocation of duties. If properly run, all the parts of the enterprise will work together. Important considerations are:

1   The need for good communication as well as good communications systems, both internal and external. The importance of these can be illustrated by considering the prime function of the 'office' within a business as the place where information is received, recorded, sorted or re-arranged, acted upon, filed and passed on. A simple example is a telephone complaint: the information will be received verbally, re-arranged on a memo pad to make it easier to deal with, linked with other information (e.g. a copy of an order), a copy of the memo retained in a complaints file, the original passed to the customer service or marketing department for action. They in turn will deal with the matter, according to the procedure laid down by their own management – this will almost certainly involve getting in touch with the customer. From the above it will be seen that every

organisation needs adequate communications systems to ensure good communication both between the 'world outside' and the organisation (external), and within the organisation (internal).

2   The use of specialists as appropriate.

3   The degree of centralisation – the selection of services to operate centrally is a vital decision ('centrally' may mean one unit doing certain work for each department or one unit working for the whole organisation).

4   The span of control, i.e. the number of staff over whom each manager or supervisor has immediate and direct control. Thus a departmental manager might have four supervisors, each of whom controls the work of a number of staff; there is no 'correct' figure for this, but between five and fifteen is considered appropriate in many organisations.

Organisation charts

In a small business with just a few employees everyone knows his role and there is direct contact between employer and staff. A formal written-down structure is not needed. However, as a business grows larger, a bigger and bigger gap is created between those involved. More people are inserted into these gaps and so the need for a formal framework becomes apparent. Thus many organisations draw up charts showing the lines of authority and responsibility. This also ensures that everyone reports to a superior.

The organisation chart illustrated might prove suitable for the head office of a large group retailing electrical and other household goods through a chain of high street branches, with its central warehouse on the same site as head office and four wholesale distribution depots each covering a number of the branches. All ordering is carried out from head office (an example of centralisation) – thus it is carrying out the wholesale function itself (see Chapter 6).

The head office departments in this example are controlled by:

The Company Secretary, who has responsibility for administration work in connection with shareholders, directors, company meetings and legal duties imposed by various Acts. He deals with the legal aspects of business functions connected with properties, insurance, contracts, etc.

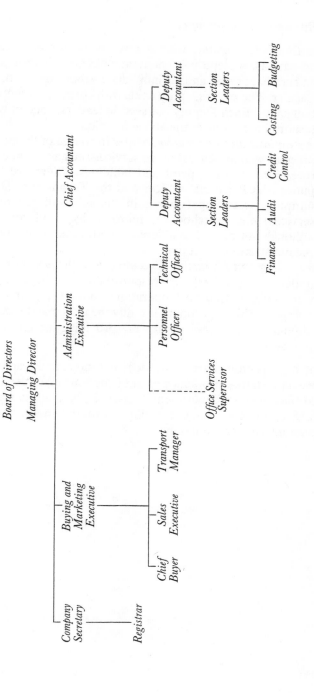

The Chief Accountant, who is responsible for all accounting operations. A Deputy Accountant looks after finance, auditing and credit control, and his immediate subordinate is the Chief Cashier. The other Deputy deals with costing, estimating and budgeting. Each Deputy has section leaders, each of whom is responsible for one of the above functions.

The Administration Executive, who is in charge of the personnel office as well as general office services such as the mail room, reception, security, plant and buildings. There are two deputies, the Personnel Officer and the Technical Officer. An Office Services Supervisor is in charge of all general office services (e.g. switchboard, reprography, mail room) and, although not ranked as a deputy head, reports directly to the Administration Executive.

The Buying and Marketing Executive with three senior officials under him (or her) has responsibility for buying, selling, warehousing, transport operations, advertising and market research. This department is really the only one directly operational – the others basically are providing indirect and support services.

The organisation chart shown does not indicate the activities of subordinate staff – in practice each of the four main departments would have its own departmental chart showing all its staff functions. Section leaders responsibilities are shown for the Chief Accountant's department only.

3

The Private Sector: Finance

The Stock Exchange

It has already been mentioned that stocks and shares (there is a purely technical difference between these two types of securities) in public limited companies can be transferred freely; basically, the shareholder is merely transferring his right to receive a proportion of the company's profits. As on an average day there are over 10 000 share transfers, it will be obvious that a 'market place' is necessary; or, to put it another way, if a market where securities could be bought and sold quickly, efficiently and under strict safeguards for the protection of investors did not exist, then many potential shareholders in public limited companies would be deterred from investing their capital. The Stock Exchange (a very old-established private institution controlled by its own elected council) is this market. There are a number of stock exchanges in various provincial towns, but as the majority of transactions are handled through the London Stock Exchange the procedure referred to below is that operating in London. Similar institutions exist in other countries (Wall Street in New York, the Bourse in Paris); but sometimes, as in Switzerland, it is the commercial banks that provide the market for transactions in securities.

It is not only securities of commercial firms that are dealt with on the Stock Exchange. There are other main types of securities:

Government and municipal loans and bonds. Governments, local authorities and other public bodies (water boards, docks and harbour boards, and so on) need to borrow money for capital expenditure – for major projects like pumping stations – which is not covered by rates and taxes. They often raise money by issuing loan stock at a fixed rate of interest. Normally the stock is 'dated': that is, it will be redeemed, or bought back, by the authority issuing the stock at a given date. An example is 12% Exchequer Stock 1999–2002 – the Treasury will choose the date to redeem.

After the stock has been issued, then, as with commercial securities, transfer is freely permissible and a considerable proportion of the work of the Stock Exchange is in the public authorities sector (around 80% of total turnover).

Interest rates will normally be a little lower than those paid by commercial fixed-interest securities, because in effect the interest payment is virtually guaranteed out of public funds.

Debenture stock issued by commercial firms. As with the public sector, these are fixed-interest loans, usually dated and normally secured on the assets of the company (really the equivalent of mortgages). If this is so, then in the event of liquidation the debenture holders have a prior claim on the cash available to the business – if any company is bankrupt, an official receiver is appointed to dispose of the assets of the business as profitably as he can. An example some years ago involved Rolls-Royce Ltd, which went into liquidation: in this case, however, because of its vital position as a manufacturer of aircraft components, the state took over some of its functions, and the car production section of the business was also saved.

Debenture holders are creditors, not shareholders, so that the interest payable to them is a charge against profits. 'Secured debentures' are the safest form of investment in a commercial firm, and interest rates will, other things being equal, be slightly lower than those paid to preference shareholders (dealt with in Chapter 2).

The reader should realise that the raising of fresh capital is not a *main* function of the Stock Exchange, though a firm of stockbrokers – see below – may be directly concerned with a special method of raising capital for small public companies known as a 'placing'. Subject to certain safeguards the issuing broker is allowed to arrange the distribution of the shares prior to the commencement of dealings. As seen above, the Stock Exchange provides a market for existing, that is, second-hand, securities, and very little money would be subscribed for a new issue of capital unless it were known beforehand that Stock Exchange dealings would take place in it after the shares had been issued. These dealings can only take place if the Stock Exchange Council has granted the company a *quotation*, or permission to deal. To secure the permission a number of stringent conditions have to be met by the company concerned, in addition to the legal requirements imposed by the Companies Acts. At present, about 8000 securities are officially quoted, their total value being nearly £400 000 million. Over 3 000 000 people directly own shares, and nearly ten times this number are investors indirectly through life assurance and pension schemes. In terms of total holdings the institutions own about half all fixed-interest stocks, as well as very considerable amounts of ordinary shares.

Stockbrokers and stockjobbers

There are two kinds of members of the London Stock Exchange: brokers and jobbers. To become a member involves satisfying the Council both about financial status and about personal integrity. In total there are about 4000 members in around 250 firms, of whom less than 20 are jobbing firms. Although firms are now permitted to become limited companies (see Chapter 2), their directors must retain unlimited personal liability; this is a protection both to clients and other member firms with whom they deal.

The stockbroker acts as an agent for the public and is paid a commission for his services. The rate varies according to the type of security and the amount involved, but overall it probably averages about 1½p in the £ on the actual cost of the shares. He is responsible for ensuring that the necessary paperwork is done in connection with the share transfer – rather more legal formality exists than with a simple contract, where mere physical exchange of the cash, goods or services may be sufficient. In addition, he has a duty to his client to ensure that he receives any dividends due to him, since in respect of transactions going through the system when a dividend is declared (see page 31) the new shareholder's name will not be recorded in the company's share register.

Brokers will have their main offices fairly close to the Stock Exchange, but they will also have a small office in the Stock Exchange.

Jobbers are principals or wholesalers in securities; they do not deal with the public direct. They are the 'risk takers' in the same way as any trader. They aim to sell at a higher price than that at which they buy; they differ from other traders in that they are expected by the rules of the Stock Exchange to deal in reasonable quantities of any quoted security, even if they are not so inclined and may, in fact, not even possess the particular security required by the buyer. The jobber knows that in the ordinary course of dealing he will have the opportunity to sell the securities he has bought or to buy in to meet a selling commitment already entered into. He will, of course, adjust his prices to encourage or discourage buyers and sellers according to the particular circumstances. In practice, jobbers tend to specialise in a particular 'market', such as industrial shares, property companies, government stocks, and so on. In every market there will be a number of jobbers dealing, and this provides the necessary rivalry to keep prices competitive.

A typical transaction

Imagine that a client has instructed his stockbroker to buy 500 £1 shares in Euroco Equipment Plc. The former knows from perusal of the financial columns of his daily newspaper (the information is derived from the Stock Exchange Daily List, which gives the average prices at which securities changed hands the previous day) that the price has varied between 115p and 121p recently, and he has told his broker not to buy if the price is above 123p – many people may, of course, leave this decision to the broker's professional judgement. The broker will contact a jobber in the appropriate market (traditionally they occupy set positions on the floor of the Stock Exchange) and ask for a price for Euroco Equipment Plc, without disclosing whether his client is a buyer or a seller. The jobber names two prices, let us say 118½p (the *bid*) and 120p (the *offer*) – that is, the jobber will buy at the lower figure and sell at the higher. Because the jobber does not know if it is to be a buying or a selling transaction, he will keep prices at a level that takes into account his unsold stock of securities in the company and the prices and quantities of earlier transactions. If the broker is not satisfied, he will ask another jobber for a price; however, having refused the first jobber, he cannot go back to him a few minutes later and necessarily expect 118½p/120p to be quoted again, for the jobber will know he did not fare better elsewhere. If we assume Jobber

No. 2 quotes 118½p/119½p, then the deal will be made as the client will be saving ½p a share.

There is a legal contract in existence from this moment, even though it has been by word of mouth; each person merely records details in a notebook and the necessary paper work is dealt with later by the respective office staffs. Readers may know of the Stock Exchange motto *Dictum meum pactum* – 'My word is my bond'.

The Stock Exchange Council provides certain central services for all member firms. Two of these are:

1 *Settlement department.* To avoid the necessity of individual payments for thousands of transactions a fortnightly settlement is made between brokers and jobbers by this department, which has now been wholly computerised. Incidentally, the client also settles with his broker at the end of the 'account period' – in effect, this gives two weeks' credit.
2 *Information services.* The Daily List has already been referred to – this is produced from details supplied by members. In addition, closed-circuit television can be rented by member firms giving prices obtained up to about an hour before for securities of certain major companies. An index figure both for London and for Wall Street is also given which shows the general overall movement of prices that day.

It has been seen that demand and supply determine price levels. Obviously good financial results from a company will stimulate demand and vice versa. However, other factors can affect prices very much, for example, information that a company has secured large orders for future delivery. The results of a leading company may affect share prices of other companies in the same field, thus good results from Marks & Spencer may increase prices of shares of other companies running chain stores as well as their own. Taxation changes, such as a change in the rate of Value Added Tax (see page 77), which may increase retail selling prices, may affect the shares of the manufacturers. Strikes and other political and economic problems may again alter share prices. Finally, shares of companies with overseas interests (say, oil companies in the Middle East) will fluctuate if there are political troubles abroad. The jobber is the key man; he is the expert who will adjust his prices so that he clears his book as quickly as he can – he does not want to be holding securities for longer than is absolutely necessary. His aim is quick turnover, since if he buys and sells in the same 'account period' he will not be called upon to pay. The reader will see that a company has no financial interest in share dealings after the initial issue – though, of course, its directors may be affected *as shareholders*; all that it is concerned with is registering the legal transfer of the shares in its share register.

The above description of the Stock Exchange has necessarily been brief. Those interested should visit the London Stock Exchange in Throgmorton Street, EC2. There is a visitors' gallery with guides in attendance, and several documentary films are shown. A number of pamphlets are also available free on application by post or visit to the public relations officer.

A typical company and its finances – a share issue

In practice, there would be little chance of having a successful issue to the public of share capital unless the business had already had a successful trading record; the public would be hardly likely to subscribe to an issue for an entirely new trading venture. Very often it is a private limited company that 'goes public' in order to raise capital for expansion; its existing shareholders will be allocated shares in the new company and, in addition, may be given priority for the purchase of extra shares up to a given limit. Alternatively, an existing public company may be endeavouring to raise additional capital, and it is this type of issue that will now be considered.

In addition to the 'public issue' – a straightforward offer of shares to the general public – another method called an 'offer for sale' is commonly used. In this a company sells shares directly to a financial institution called an issuing house (see page 86), which then disposes of them to the public. However, from the public's point of view there is no real difference – it is basically a procedural matter.

Imagine that the capital position of Oreco Equipment Plc, successful office machinery manufacturers, is as follows:

	Nominal £	Issued £
8% £1 Cumulative preference shares	400 000	300 000
£1 Ordinary shares	2 000 000	1 200 000
		1 500 000
Reserves		300 000
		£1 800 000

The reserves of £300 000 represent the portion of the net profits that has been 'ploughed back' into the business, that is, not paid out to shareholders as dividends, since the company commenced trading. It therefore follows that the company must have net assets (i.e. total assets less creditors) of £1 800 000. These assets will not, of course, all be in cash – in fact, the total cash may be quite low. The main assets are likely to be:

Freehold premises; plant and machinery; motor vehicles; office equipment; unsold stock of goods; unused stock of raw materials; debtors and cash.

If the amounts owing (liabilities) are deducted from the total of these assets, a figure of £1 800 000 will be reached. A statement setting out the assets and liabilities of a business is called its *balance sheet* (see Chapter 11).

The company is now going to raise £600 000 (£500 000 from the issue of ordinary shares and £100 000 from preference shares) and therefore makes the necessary preliminary arrangements with an issuing house or with the new issues department of one of the major commercial banks. The prospectus is prepared, setting out in statutory form the details of the company's activities, and the public are invited to submit applications.

The Companies Acts stipulate that if an abridged prospectus is published in the press, then an application form may not be included; this is to ensure that everyone applying for shares has an opportunity of reading the whole prospectus, which is normally distributed by stockbrokers and banks.

A wide variety of persons or organisations is likely to be interested in the issue; generally speaking, the small investor will not be attracted by the preference shares. These have dividend priority over the ordinary shares, though in good years the latter will usually pay a higher rate of dividend, and may well appeal to the 'institutional' investor to whom safety and known rate of income is important – these have already been referred to.

If the issue is oversubscribed, and this is quite likely if the economy is booming and the company is one that has had a successful trading record over a number of years and has expansion potential, then the issuing house or board of directors will decide on the method of allotment – this will be done on an equitable basis. As cash is normally asked for in full with applications, this will mean that surplus money will have to be returned. After the whole £600 000 worth of shares has been issued, the position will be as follows:

	Nominal £	Issued £
8% £1 Cumulative preference shares	400 000	400 000
£1 Ordinary shares	2 000 000	1 700 000
		2 100 000
Reserves		300 000
		£2 400 000

The £600 000 cash received will, of course, increase the company's liquid resources by this sum, so that there will now be net assets of £2 400 000. It should be realised that the company has to use this new money profitably because it now has more shareholders (i.e. more mouths to feed with a share of profits). Although it may not do so immediately, the company will set a target for the extra profit it hopes to make. It will probably aim annually for at least 12% (of the £600 000), that is, an extra £72 000. The dividend calculation below shows that the annual 'cost' of this new money, assuming a 10% reward to ordinary shareholders, will be:

8% of £100 000	8 000
10% of £500 000	50 000
	£58 000

Once the company's extra profits are more than £72000 per year the raising of the £600000 has been justified.

The dividend

Let us assume that several years later the company makes a net profit after tax of £267000. The directors decide to plough back £65000 and to pay the remainder as dividend, thus:

Preference shareholders	8% of £400000	32000
Ordinary shareholders	10% of £1700000	170000
		202000
Transferred to reserves		65000
		£267000

The company's net assets this year must therefore have increased by £65000. Of course, the ordinary dividend may well have been higher or lower – the figure of 10% has merely been used as an illustration.

A shareholder who bought 500 ordinary £1 shares will receive a gross dividend of £50 (in practice, income tax is deducted). At some later date he may decide to sell; let us assume he obtains 110p a share. The new shareholder will have paid out £550 (500 × 110p) – commission has been ignored. If in the following year an ordinary dividend of 10% is again declared, the new owner will only receive 10% of the nominal value, that is, 10% of £500 = £50. As was pointed out when dealing with the Stock Exchange, the company is not concerned with the price at which shares change hands.

The new owner's yield or return will be:

Dividend

$$\frac{50}{550} \times 100 = 9\% \text{ approximately}$$

Capital invested

One must therefore be wary of assuming that, if a company declares a dividend of $x\%$, all its shareholders will have received a return of

$x\%$ on their investment; if the £1 share cost £2, then the return becomes $\frac{1}{2}x\%$.

(Note: Although in the case of Oreco Equipment Plc dealt with in this chapter an issue of £600 000 was illustrated, in practice a 'public issue' or 'offer for sale' nowadays is likely to be for at least several million pounds.)

4

The Public Sector; Co-operative Societies; Trade Unions

The public sector

The state has for a very long time, either directly or through subordinate bodies such as local authorities, provided various social and other central services for the benefit of the community at large paid for out of various forms of taxation. Examples are education, sanitation, highways and defence. However, in addition, there has been increasing participation by the state in the provision of goods and services where the customer makes a direct payment for value received; in other words, this is the 'state as a trader'. Early examples were the Port of London Authority (1908), the British Broadcasting Corporation (1927), and the London Passenger Transport Board (1933). With one exception (the BBC was created by Royal Charter), an Act of Parliament was passed in each case, setting up a public corporation with an appointed board responsible for the operation of the particular industry. These corporations, though publicly owned, differed from government departments, which with a number of exceptions (the Post Office until 1969, the Stationery Office, the Forestry Commission, the Royal Mint) never acted as traders in the above sense. Trading services provided by local authorities are referred to in Chapter 16.

It was during the time of the 1945–50 Labour government that the state began to participate on a much greater scale than hitherto in business activities and nationalised a number of the basic public utility industries. In each case, the state compulsorily acquired the industry from its previous owners – who in some cases had been subject to some form of state control anyway, such as the four railway companies and the Bank of England – and paid them compensation. The chief industries concerned were:

Industry	Pre-1945 position
Coal	Privately owned collieries.
Railways	Four major privately owned companies, each with an area monopoly granted by parliament.
Electricity	Some undertakings owned privately, others run by local authorities. A national 'grid' fed them.
Gas	Some private, some local authority ownership.
Road Transport	Very large numbers of privately owned businesses.
Airlines (British Airways)	Civil aviation strictly controlled during 1939 to 1945 and immediately after the war; pre-1939 industry was comparatively small.

In some cases, such as road transport, part of the industry remained in private hands; in 1951 steel was nationalised, almost immediately denationalised by a Conservative government and partly renationalised by a Labour government in 1966. There have been a number of basic changes in the road transport position since public ownership first came about (see Chapter 12). The Central Bank, the Bank of England, also became a public corporation, though City of London financial interests still retain some considerable measure of influence. In addition, several public corporations were established in 'new' industries, examples being the Atomic Energy Authority and the Independent Television Authority, to control the activities of the independent television companies. With the advent of commercial radio, the latter has become the Independent Broadcasting Authority. It was seen earlier that a corporation is a body that is given in law an artificial life as distinct from that of the individuals forming it.

The justification for public ownership
Unfortunately, this has become over the years an acute political issue and many people think of it in terms of:

Private sector	versus	*Public sector*
Private owners insist on efficiency in the interest of their profits		Inefficient as profit motive does not exist

This generalisation is not only an absurd oversimplification but also patently untrue. There are efficient and inefficient fields both in the public and in the private sectors.

The first post-war Labour government was deeply committed to nationalisation in the public interest. Its argument was that in certain basic industries consideration of the public interest was of greater importance than the need to make private profit; that certain services should be available to all (including public transport in remote areas); and that where profits could be made these should accrue to the state. Other arguments in favour of public ownership were as follows:

1   It was only by concentration into larger units that the economies of large-scale production could be made possible, and this was unlikely under private ownership.
2   As monopolies had of necessity to exist (for example, the railways), these should be in state rather than in private hands.
3   Labour relations, particularly in coal mining, had been very bad during the inter-war years, and it would be quite impossible to secure trade union co-operation without public ownership.
4   Particularly during 1939 to 1945, the basic industries had been starved of capital investment, and private enterprise would be unable or unwilling to provide sufficient capital for redevelopment purposes in an increasingly technological age.
5   In some fields, such as atomic energy, the need for security made complete state control necessary.

The main arguments against nationalisation are that unless there are clearly identifiable owners, with a profit motive for ensuring that a business is run properly, then inefficiency will result because the employees, who generally have more security of tenure than in private employment, will not give of their best; that unless there is the spur of competition, then again efficiency will suffer; that the mere creation of vast public undertakings means considerably less flexibility than would be found in smaller units.

However, the major political parties in this country accept that to a greater or lesser extent, for the reasons given above, public ownership is necessary in certain circumstances. But the Conservative Party takes the view that the public sector should be kept as small as possible, and that where industries can be run by private enterprise profitably this should be done. Certainly there was no great move towards denationalisation by successive Conservative governments from 1951 to 1964, although the 1970 to 1974 administration did sell back to private enterprise a few of the more profitable activities of some of the public corporations.

The Conservative administration elected in 1979 and re-elected in 1983 had as a major aim the restoration of market forces throughout the economy. Accordingly it introduced a policy of 'privatisation'. This return of industries, assets and activities to the private sector took a number of forms, including the sale to private individuals of shareholdings in former nationalised industries; the disposal of government shareholdings in companies; as well as the abolition of statutory monopolies, thus allowing private enterprise to compete. The government felt that implementing this policy would allow private enterprise managers to choose their strategy without political interference. A secondary government objective was to provide a boost to wider share ownership; another was to improve national revenue income from the sale of the assets involved and to reduce the public sector borrowing requirement.

Examples of privatisation were the sale of a majority shareholding in the exploration and production business of the British National Oil Corporation, Britoil Plc; the sale of shares in British Aerospace Plc, formerly the nationalised British Aircraft Corporation; the sale of the government shareholding in British Petroleum Plc, generally known as BP, which netted £276 million. The National Freight Company, formerly a nationalised industry, was purchased by a consortium of its managers and employees and is now the National Freight Corporation, a limited company: special arrangements exist to prevent sale of shares to non-employees.

In 1981 British Telecom was set up as a separate public corporation to run some services formerly operated by the Post Office. At the same time some of the monopoly powers were removed and the industry secretary was given powers to license others to run certain telecommunication systems. In addition he was empowered to allow private operators to provide some postal services, such as express mail.

Control of public corporations
In the same way that the objects of a limited company are included in its Memorandum of Association (page 18), so the Act of Parliament setting up a public corporation defines its powers and functions, and sets up its general organisation. Corporations are given more freedom than government departments and are not servants or agents of the Crown in the way that government departments are; their employees are not civil servants. In each case, a minister takes general responsibility for the particular industry, but the extent of his power varies. However, in all cases he appoints the board and has power to give 'directions of a general nature' as to how the industry should be run, but he does not interfere with day-to-day management. In many ways, the board can be compared to a board of directors of a company; it has, however, more responsibility and less freedom of action. Public corporations were created in this way because it was realised that they needed a high degree of freedom from direct parliamentary and ministerial control to enable them to operate as far as possible on commercial lines. In practice, the responsible minister is kept fully informed and major policy decisions are reached only after consultation with him. For example, British Airways would not decide to buy an American instead of a British aircraft without government approval; similarly, the government would have to be consulted about the fuel to be used at power stations. Annually, each public corporation presents its report and accounts to parliament through the responsible minister; there is, however, only limited time available for debate.

A Select Committee of Nationalised Industries was set up in 1956, and it has held a number of inquiries into the management of particular industries. In many ways it has proved effective in maintaining broad general control by parliament. To protect the consumers' interests a consultative committee has been set up in most nationalised industries to deal with consumers' views and complaints: one example is the Post Office Users' Council.

Finance
In respect of the industries that were nationalised, fixed-interest stock (page 26) was issued as compensation to the private shareholder. This has meant that these industries have had to meet heavy yearly interest payments whether there was a profit or a loss; in this sense, this type of interest payment can be likened to debenture interest (page 26), which again is a 'charge'. Originally, long-term capital was raised by the issue of fixed-interest stocks, but in recent years the Treasury has advanced money direct to the industries.

As part of the privatisation policy already referred to, some private capital would be introduced into existing public corporations, for example into the National Bus Company, as well as British Telecom.

The government exercises a broad control over all new capital expenditure. In the case of a number of these public corporations, the Acts establishing them stated that the industry should pay its way, 'taking one year with another'. In practice, although industries like gas and electricity have tended to achieve this goal, several of the others, such as the railways, have had enormous deficits over the years (see Chapter 12). In recent years, a more precise goal has been set for each industry: each has been given a financial target representing a fixed percentage of capital invested.

The following statistics give a general picture of the enormous size of the major nationalised industries in 1980–1: the total net assets of the six largest public sector industries (Post Office, British Telecom, rail, gas, coal, steel) was about £25000 million; the total turnover was about £30000 million. The British National Oil Corporation has not been included because of its part privatisation.

Co-operative societies

These will be looked at in their role as retail traders in Chapter 5; here they are considered as a distinctive form of business organisation which cannot really be included in either the private or the public sector. However, co-operative societies can be said to resemble the public corporation in perhaps one way – they aim to replace private enterprise. The aim of the original co-operative movement was to replace the private enterprise commercial order by a co-operative commonwealth.

A co-operative society can be described as a business undertaking owned and operated by a voluntary association of persons or organisations in order to provide themselves with work and wages, or with goods and services. Although co-operative ownership is as old as human history, the modern movement had its origins in the nineteenth century (Rochdale 1844); it was the wretched conditions of the lowest income groups that led to the establishment of the movement. The principles of the Rochdale Society of Equitable Pioneers can be summarised thus:

a open membership,
b democratic control,
c distribution of trading surplus in proportion to purchases,
d limited interest on capital,
e religious and political neutrality,
f cash trading only,
g promotion of education.

The Rochdale store was started by the members subscribing small amounts at a low rate of interest – 3½%. All had an equal vote in deciding policy (one man one vote – *not* one share one vote). Later, anyone was able to become a member by paying 1 shilling deposit on a £5 share, the balance being paid in gradually out of the dividend. The movement grew slowly and in 1852 obtained a recognised legal status. Wholesale societies were set up as a result of an Act of 1862 which permitted co-operatives to become members of each other, and from this date there was rapid expansion. By 1881 there were 1000 retail societies and 500 000 members; by 1960 this had grown to 13 million, although the number of societies, which had reached 1400 by the 1910s, had fallen to about 200 by 1981 owing to amalgamation. Each retail society is, of course, a separate legal unit. The problems of the retail societies are discussed in Chapter 5.

Legal status

Most societies are now registered under the Industrial and Provident Societies Acts (consolidated into the 1965 Act). Although no

	No of members	*Capital*	*Control*
SOLE TRADER	1 owner	Provided by owner	Wholly by owner
PARTNERSHIP	2–20 with a few exceptions	Subscribed by partners in agreed proportions	Divided among partners by arrangement – partnership share only transferable by agreement
PRIVATE LIMITED COMPANY (Ltd)	Minimum 2; no maximum	Public issue forbidden, but raising of additional capital now easier	Shareholders elect board of directors (minimum of 1). Right to transfer shares *may* be restricted by Articles of Association
PUBLIC LIMITED COMPANY (Plc)	Minimum 2; no maximum	May be raised by public issue or offer for sale. Minimum capital £50000	Shares transferable without restriction (Stock Exchange). Shareholders elect board of directors
PUBLIC CORPORATION (nationalised)	None – state-owned	(*a*) Assets compulsorily acquired from private owners. (*b*) Public issue of fixed interest stock. (*c*) Provided by Exchequer (but refer to earlier notes)	Responsible minister appoints salaried board. He exercises general (not detailed) control
CO-OPERATIVE	No maximum	Any member of public may buy shares up to £5000 maximum	Management committee elected by shareholders. Shares not transferable, but capital can be withdrawn or added to at any time

Profits	Liability of members	Acts of Parliament
Belong to owner	Unlimited liability for business debts	None
Divided equally unless agreement to the contrary	Unlimited liability – partners bear losses usually in profit-sharing ratio. Limited partnerships possible but uncommon – at least one partner must accept unlimited liability	Partnership Act 1890. Limited Partnership Act 1907
Preference shareholders – fixed % dividend. Ordinary shareholders – variable % dividend	Shareholders have no additional liability after shareholding fully paid (small number of unlimited companies)	Companies Acts 1948/1981
Preference shareholders – fixed % dividend. Ordinary shareholders – variable % dividend	Shareholders have no additional liability after shareholding fully paid	
Can be used to reduce charges or to finance expansion, or paid to Exchequer to reduce taxation	Not applicable – state accepts full liability	Individual Acts (e.g. Gas Act 1948)
(a) Fixed interest (usually 5% on capital invested). (b) Dividend may sometimes be paid based on purchases. 'Instant' dividend (trading stamps) schemes operate	No liability after shareholding fully paid	Industrial and Provident Societies Acts

positive definition of a co-operative society is given, the 1965 Act states that a co-operative does *not* include a society that carries on business with the object of making profits mainly for the payment of interest on money invested or lent. A society thus registered is an association of shareholding members with limited liability, and it is a corporate body with a right to sue and be sued. The Rules of a society (corresponding to the Articles of Association of a limited company) must be approved by the Registrar of Friendly Societies. Total share capital is unlimited, but the maximum shareholding is £5000 per annum per member and, unlike limited companies, shares are withdrawable on demand and are not transferable. Investment in a co-operative society's shares can therefore be treated like a savings bank account. Interest is paid at a fixed rate, usually 5%. Some societies continue the one-time universal practice of paying a dividend to members based on their purchases. Many have abandoned this on the grounds of the high administrative costs involved; instead they attempt to reduce prices to all shoppers.

Management and control
Power ultimately resides in the ordinary general meeting of members, which elects a committee of management to be responsible for the business of the society. In the larger societies much of the detailed business of the management committee is done in sub-committee, for instance trading, finance, and so on.

The largest society in the movement is the Co-operative Wholesale Society (incorporating the old Scottish Wholesale Society); in addition, there are two other societies, one of which engages in the production of tea and other commodities, and the other of which controls the Co-operative Insurance Society. Apart from the amalgamation of the CWS and the SCWS several years ago the basic structure of the wholesale societies has hardly changed in ninety years. Originally, they were created to serve the retail societies as wholesale agents, but over the years they have extended their operations to include large-scale manufacturing, insurance, banking and many other fields of commercial activity. The CWS is owned and controlled by the member societies on a democratic basis. Directors are elected by the member societies as shareholders, and their voting strength is decided by the amount of their purchases, not by the amount of the shares they hold – the minimum amount of shareholding is determined by the membership of the individual society, a minimum of one £5 share for each two members.

Trade unions

Trade unions are in a special category: technically they are neither unincorporations, like sole traders, nor incorporated bodies, like limited companies. Their precise legal position is outside the scope of a commerce text. Suffice it to say that to be eligible for registration under the 1975 Employment Protection Act a trade union must show that it consists wholly or mainly of employees and that its principal purposes include the regulation of relationships between employee and employer. Unions are organised either by occupation or by industry, or on a combination of both principles. In some firms membership of a relevant union is compulsory as a result of an agreement between employer and union – the 'closed shop'.

There are over 400 trade unions in Britain, with a total membership of twelve or thirteen millions; that is, about 40% of the total labour force. Over two-thirds of the unions have a very small membership, whilst the dozen or so really large unions enrol between them two out of every three unionists. Names like the Transport and General Workers Union, with two million members, will be known to readers; it is worth noting that the greatest increase in membership in the past few decades has been amongst non-manual employees. Of these unions the largest is the National and Local Government Officers Association (NALGO), with 750000 members.

The national centre of the movement is the Trades Union Congress, to which unions representing over 90% of all unionists are affiliated. It deals with all general questions which concern unions both nationally and internationally, and, through membership of the National Economic Development Council, participates in discussions relating to the national economy.

Readers wishing to know more about trade unionism are referred to the excellent summaries in either *Descriptive Economics* by Professor Colin Harbury (Pitman) or *Britain – An Official Handbook* published annually by the government Stationery Office (HMSO) and available in any municipal reference library.

5

Retailing

The retail customer

One half of all expenditure in the United Kingdom goes through shops. In real terms total retail sales have increased by 10% in five years; currently it is about £1000 yearly per head of population. About one person in ten is employed in retail distribution. What, then, is the retail trade? It is the section of trading involved in selling goods and services to the customer, the man (or woman or child) in the street who is buying them for the personal use of his household – the final consumer. So it does not include goods and services purchased by one business from another – for example, an engineering firm buying equipment to enable it to manufacture component parts, or a refrigerator manufacturer purchasing accessories for use in his product. These are called producer's goods.

The retailer is part of the chain of distribution. Goods may have reached him direct from the manufacturer, or via a wholesaler (a bulk buyer). Either way, he is the last link in the chain. His task is to provide the consumer with the goods and services he wants

a   at the right time,
b   in the right quantities and form,
c   in the right place.

Thus the consumer wants to be able to buy apples in December (though they may have been harvested in September) in 1 or 2 lb quantities suitably graded, and furthermore he prefers to be offered a choice of product.

Retailing has certain basic characteristics which have influenced the form it has taken. In the first place, the customer has only *limited time*, and for 'convenience' goods (everyday items like food, household sundries and newspapers) he does not normally wish to travel far; but note that for 'shopping' goods (clothes and comparatively expensive durables such as furniture and television sets) he is generally prepared to 'shop around'. So, particularly for convenience goods, he prefers to be able to shop fairly near his home. Thus there are vast numbers of shops in this country (about one for every 140 persons – over 350 000 retail selling points in all). Secondly, he likes *variety of choice*; often it may well be the influence of advertising that has persuaded him to demand brand A rather than brand X, even if basically they are the same. The retailer must still try to satisfy him and to stock, whenever possible, several varieties of the same article.

Another characteristic is that the *physical size of the purchase is limited*, partly because of transport and storage difficulties in the home, and partly because the consumer's cash is limited and is likely to be more available to him on a weekly basis.

Again, we do not spread our shopping evenly throughout the day, week or year. There are certain peak times for different types of shops and different types of goods: lunchtimes in central areas, Saturdays for those unable to shop in the week, Christmas for gifts, and so on. It may become necessary to employ part-time staff (which can be both expensive and inefficient for these periods). Conversely, there are occasions when staff are underemployed (for example Monday is a comparatively quiet day in many trades) and therefore the employer receives little financial return in relation to his expenses incurred.

Finally, the consumer's ideas on fashion and his taste change at frequent intervals (particularly in lines like clothing); again, the influence of large-scale advertising may cause this.

The effect of the above characteristics is to ensure that retailing facilities are often provided at relatively high cost. In many trades the retailer, particularly if his business is a small one, may need to add as much as one half or more to the price he himself paid for the goods. In theory, if the consumer were compelled by law to buy certain standard brands in certain areas at certain times of the day, week or year in certain quantities, retail prices would drop. However, this state of affairs is hardly likely to become a reality in our society! It is, of course, worth mentioning that, particularly in the last ten years, the large-scale retailers (supermarkets and multiples) have in some instances deliberately limited the number of brands or styles offered to customers (tinned and packeted foods, and shoes are two examples).

The retailer's functions can be summarised as follows:

1   He needs to be able to anticipate consumer demand.
2   He has to store goods in sufficient quantities to enable him to have stocks available for sale. This necessitates his having funds to buy in bulk.
3   Even though in many areas retailing goods arrive at the retailer's premises packed and ready for sale, he may still be concerned to some extent with grading, packing and sorting.
4   He must be willing and able to assist his customers in selecting appropriate goods for their needs – though, again, this function is not as important as it was.
5   He may need to give credit and, in the case of bulky goods, may have to arrange delivery.

Types of retail business

Numerically, the small organisations dominate the retail trade. Some 350 000 outlets are controlled by over 230 000 organisations, so the vast majority must be 'one-shop' organisations. Shop location is of prime importance; as has already been seen, shops selling convenience goods must be widely distributed while those selling shopping goods of higher unit value will be fewer in number but in centres readily accessible to considerable numbers of persons. In the last twenty-five years there has been much change in the pattern of retailing: self-service, mail order and machine vending have all grown in importance; supermarkets have sprung up all over the country; hypermarkets are now beginning to appear; the shopping precinct in the centre of the town has been created.

Whereas in manufacturing specialisation has been found to be the most satisfactory method of production, in retailing two forces have been at work in equal and opposite directions: on the one hand, retailers in general have felt it advantageous to diversify because this is likely to increase turnover without materially altering fixed expenses; on the other hand, in certain trades, specialisation (whether in the range of goods sold or in the class of customer catered for) has been found to be profitable. So the pattern of retailing is a very complicated one; diversification v. specialisation is the order of battle.

Small-scale retailers

These may be stallholders in established street markets; itinerant traders selling either from door to door or from a barrow; mobile vans (largely in country areas); unit shops (a single shop with one or two owners); or, finally, a small group of shops (but not large enough to be given the classification of 'multiple' – see below). Small-scale retailers account for over one third of the total retail sales in the country, including three quarters of confectionery, tobacco and newspapers. The vast majority are sole traders or partnerships (see Chapter 2). They can be divided into two main categories: (i) general and (ii) speciality stores. For the latter a certain amount of craft knowledge may be needed, and it is in this sort of business that the 'personal service element' becomes important; examples are hairdressers, florists, jewellers, photographic dealers. Nowadays, many owners of stores in the 'general' category have (and, in fact, need) little knowledge of the particular trade because of the growing tendency for branding and prepacking, goods largely being sold on the strength of the manufacturer's advertising.

The unit shop's share of the total retail market has dropped very considerably in the last few decades because of growing competition from large-scale businesses. The small retailer has less capital to improve premises and layout, he cannot buy on such favourable terms as large-scale firms, and he often lacks the expertise of the specialist buyer or other technical and professional staff that the large organisation can employ. Nevertheless, the percentage share of sales has not dropped to the extent many anticipated years ago. In 1947 the small retailer had about 65% of total retail sales; now it is perhaps 35%. The reasons for this lower than expected reduction are:

1 As already mentioned, he may be skilled in his particular trade.
2 Often he is in a convenient position in the suburbs away from a main shopping centre; or he may be in a rural area.

3   Although he cannot get bulk-buying advantages (but see 5), he can often sell comparatively cheaply because of low overhead expenses. He is also likely to use 'cash-and-carry' warehouses (see page 61).

4   Many customers still like 'personal service' from the 'corner shop'. However, the importance of this is often very much overemphasised.

5   Many small retailers, particularly in food products, now buy in cooperation with other retailers; purchasing and distribution networks (generally wholesaler sponsored) have been set up which buy in bulk on their behalf – examples are Mace, Wavyline and Spar (Society for Protection of the Average Retailer). In addition to bulk buying of food, favourable terms can also be obtained in the purchase of paper bags, special-offer notices, shop fittings and so forth. Mace, the largest voluntary group, has over 30 wholesaler and 5000 retailer members, and more than 50 depots.

6   Finally, it is worth mentioning that there is still a keen desire on the part of many to be self-employed, even though it may be a financial sacrifice. Inland Revenue returns show that the average net income of the unit shopkeeper is perhaps £100 per week. Even allowing for tax avoidance and possibly evasion, this is hardly attractive!

Department stores
The characteristic of this type of retailing unit is that goods are segregated into a number of different departments, each normally under the control of its own specialist manager, who is himself subject to overriding central control. In effect, a department store is a series of retail shops housed in one building, all enjoying access to a number of services supplied for the benefit of all departments – accountancy, advertising, delivery, and so on. It is difficult to decide at what point an ordinary retail business becomes a department store, but if the definition in the census of distribution is taken it is an establishment with a minimum of twenty-five staff and a minimum of five departments (including substantial sales in clothing). William Whiteley, one of the pioneers in this form of retailing, boasted that he could supply anything from a 'pin to an elephant'. The telegraphic address of a very well-known London store before

the abolition of the telegram service was 'Everything, London', and this store is reputed to have delivered for some years a small Hovis loaf to a lady in Brighton several times a week. The UK has some hundreds of departmental stores which in total account for about 5% of retail turnover, the vast majority of which is earned by the six largest groups (the House of Fraser, owning outlets like Harrods and Selfridges, is responsible for over a quarter of total sales).

In general, department stores have not done particularly well in the past forty years, and their share of retail trade has remained fairly constant during this period. A department store has to be in an easily accessible, recognised main shopping centre, with good public transport and car-parking facilities. These high street sites are expensive to maintain and little can be done to reduce these costs. Turnover must be maintained at a high rate, and to induce the customer to spend as much as possible they are likely to provide expensive facilities, such as a car park, rest rooms, luxury carpeting and furnishings. Again, there is as yet limited self-service – this is deliberate policy, as the appeal of these stores is the quality of their services (though it is worth mentioning that many continental department stores have reversed this policy successfully in recent years). Stores will normally offer several forms of credit; may provide 'free' delivery over a large area (paid for by all the customers, of course!); may run some small departments at a loss (such as books) and have a liberal policy in exchanging goods. All this tends to increase operating costs, so prices are often higher than those of the small retailers or the multiple stores. Many customers, however, consider the better and bigger choice of goods compensates for this.

Multiple stores
This type of retail unit consists of a number of retail shops (ten is the accepted minimum) owned by one firm. Their names are household words: Curry's, Dolcis, W. H. Smith, and so on. Some are nationwide chains, others concentrate in a smaller area. In recent years, particularly in food retailing, the multiples have established chains of supermarkets (such as Sainsbury's), and these are dealt with later in this chapter.

The multiple shop normally sells the same range of goods in each one of its branches; in recent years there has been the diversification already mentioned and a wider range is stocked (for example, shoe stores selling socks and tights, tailors dealing in shirts and ties). Multiple stores are usually established in main-road positions, but in suburbs as well as town centres, because a large turnover is needed; often they obtain shops in new shopping parades and precincts where the small retailer cannot pay the high rentals demanded.

The shops of the 'chain' are under central control; usually they are standardised in layout and the goods sold are supplied from a central warehouse. Thus the firm buys in great bulk and can employ highly experienced buyers. Each shop is in charge of a skilled manager, who may have only limited authority; for example, he cannot vary shop hours or staff rates of pay and, although some discretion may be given him as far as perishable foods are concerned, he does not fix selling prices. It should be noted that some multiples have their own manufacturing units (for example Boots the Chemists).

Their share of the total retail trade has increased very quickly; in fact, the loss of total share suffered by the unit retailer has mainly gone to the multiple store, which at present is responsible for over one third of all retail sales. This success is by no means entirely attributable to the economies of large-scale buying. Careful attention to the techniques of good management has a considerable effect. Branch managers can concentrate on selling because there are other skilled persons dealing with a variety of other aspects – marketing policy, stock control, staff training, advertising, and so on; the unit retailer can hardly match this expertise. Furthermore, costs are reduced by limiting both the retail services provided (for example no credit or delivery except for consumer durables) and the range of choice available. An example of the latter restriction is seen in the selling of shoes, where stock control is wholly computerised: the large multiples in this field quite ruthlessly withdraw a particular style, or even certain sizes in that style, from the whole chain or from an individual shop if sales do not reach a certain level.

Although the multiple is found in virtually all areas of distribution, it plays a bigger part in some fields – for instance, food, clothing, footwear, chemists, off-licences, radio and electrical goods. In some trades, such as newsagents and tobacconists, confectionery, perishable goods and the motor trade, multiples are responsible for a fairly small proportion of total sales.

Variety chain stores

Perhaps if the names Marks & Spencer and Woolworth are mentioned here, a detailed definition becomes superfluous. Their significant feature is that they sell a wider range of goods in one establishment than the general multiples do without there being any definite dividing line between departments. However, as the pattern of retailing has changed the division between these stores and large multiples has become less distinct and statistics now often class the variety chain stores as specialist multiples.

As with all large stores, they need to be in good shopping centres, and several shops are often adjacent to each other. Goods are on open display; there is limited service; profit margins expressed as percentages tend to be low (they rely on high value of sales and quick turnover); and many of the goods sold are manufactured to the chain's special requirements and bear their own trademark (St Michael, Winfield, and so on). As with multiples, there is central management control. In their early days these stores sold only very cheap standard goods: Marks & Spencer's was dubbed the Penny Bazaar at the turn of the century and up to the Second World War most of their goods were priced at around 5 shillings (25p), while Woolworth's sold nothing over 6*d* (2½p). In the last decade they have diversified considerably both in range of goods and in prices, and one major chain is now granting hire-purchase facilities on purchases of durables. Generally, they have provided tough competition for the department store.

Co-operative retail societies

Their structure as units of business ownership has already been dealt with in Chapter 4. It is difficult to consider them as a separate entity in the field of retailing because they operate as multiples, department stores and supermarkets. There are about 180 societies (there have been many amalgamations in recent years); some are mammoth enterprises, others quite small, controlling perhaps a score of shops. Overall, they possess share capital of more than £250 million and have more than a quarter of a million employees. Each society is independently operated by an elected management committee, but the day-to-day operations are in the hands of professional paid staff. Anyone can become a member by taking a £1 share (maximum holding £5000) on which a fixed interest is paid, normally 5% per annum; in addition, a dividend, originally paid once or twice a year to members only, but now often given in trading stamps, based on purchases is, in some societies, allowed to all customers. Vast numbers of their customers today are non-members, and even though members get a slight cash advantage in redemption of trading stamps the material advantages of membership are small. Furthermore, because of the comparatively low rate of interest paid on fixed capital, some societies have had difficulty in attracting new capital for development purposes.

Although many societies concentrate on foodstuffs and other necessities such as coal, many operate department stores selling the same wide range of goods as their commercial-enterprise rivals. Their share of all retail sales dropped from 11% to 6% between 1961 and 1980, though in food it is about twice this figure. The movement has always had political links with the Labour Party, and some of their sales – but nowadays a reducing proportion – have always been achieved on a loyalty basis from political sympathisers (it is important to remember that the movement was founded over a century ago in an attempt to improve shopping standards for a wretchedly poor working class).

In recent years there have been strenuous efforts to reverse the slow decline of the co-operative movement; amalgamations have taken place, uneconomic factories have been closed, marketing methods improved and generally attempts made to better their public image. This policy has had the effect, since 1975, of largely stopping the decline in trade, though whether their share of the total retail trade will increase in the face of dynamic competition from the multiple-store groups remains to be seen.

Supermarkets and self-service

It has already been stated that it is becoming increasingly difficult to classify all retail selling points into fixed compartments; it is the development of the supermarkets and self-service stores that has been responsible. Self-service (originally introduced in the USA seventy years ago but not seen in the UK until the Second World War) may be practised by a small sole trader, by multiples, supermarkets and variety chain stores. Supermarkets may be part of a large multiple chain, or in some cases may be a single unit or part of a small group. Furthermore, the range of goods sold in them is in some instances so wide that it is difficult to divide them into the recognised groupings, such as groceries and provisions, household goods, other food retailing, and so on. Some supermarkets now have a completely separate department for wines and spirits or for durables.

By definition, supermarkets are stores with a sales area of over 2000 square feet (180 square metres), operating largely on a self-service basis and with three or more checkout points (incidentally, it was the co-operative movement that introduced these – and self-service – into this country). Because of their policy of stocking a wide range of largely prepacked and easily identifiable goods, often branded, at generally keen prices, they have captured an increasing proportion of the market, particularly in the food trade; it is anticipated that within a few years supermarkets and self-service will be responsible for about 90% of food sales. There are at present about 6000 supermarkets, and this figure is expected to double eventually. The ending of resale price maintenance, whereby the manufacturer could legally fix the selling price of goods, enabled the large-scale retailing organisation to enter into a price-cutting war, and this factor has been partly responsible for their increase in trade.

Nevertheless, it is not just a simple matter of:

Bulk buying→lower retail prices→higher turnover.

Skilled top-level management becomes increasingly important as organisations increase in size and complexity, and some of our best-run groups pay a great deal of attention to this area.

The trend to greater size has led to the introduction of superstores and hypermarkets; the former has a minimum 8000 square feet (2500 square metres) of selling space, and the latter twice this figure (i.e. nearly the size of the playing area of a football pitch). Though they are primarily designed for those with cars, it is government policy to encourage their development within urban areas, preferably within shopping centres – thus making them accessible to those without cars.

The massive shopping centre with a very wide range of shops selling every sort of goods and services has appeared too. There is already one with 1 million square feet (300000 square metres) of shops and 150 acres of service area. To put these figures in perspective, the former figure means an area about ¾ mile (1.2 km) by ½ mile (.8 km) and the latter, approximately 75 football pitches! There may be perhaps 130 shops in a covered shopping precinct, with 6000 parking spaces.

Discount stores
These are large stores selling furniture and other durables, often established in a warehouse-type building with poor customer facilities, whose aim is to sell at the lowest possible price on a cash-and-carry basis. As yet, this type of retailing is fairly new, but the ending of resale price maintenance (see above) encouraged growth. Already there are some drive-in discount stores for the benefit of the ever-increasing number of motorists; at least one of the large supermarket chains is interested in development in this field.

Mail order firms
This perhaps is the best example of the elimination of the retailer by the wholesaler. There has been an enormous growth in this type of selling in the last thirty years; total turnover has increased many times in this period. The vast majority of the trade is controlled by six or seven large organisations – often operating through subsidiary companies – who obtain customers through large-scale advertising and by operating through local agents – mainly women working part-time on commission, canvassing, handling orders, distributing goods and collecting cash. In recent years mail order firms have considerably increased both the quality and the range of goods sold, and the whole business has gone up the social scale. Virtually all sales are on a credit basis. The availability of reliable Post Office services in the area of both transport of goods and remittance services (see Chapter 10) has been of much assistance to the trade. Other factors responsible for the increasing popularity of mail order are the 'comfort' elements (e.g. no transport difficulties) and the even greater proportion of married women at work. Although the firms (household names like Great Universal Stores and Littlewoods) save on the traditional retailing costs, their prices are not particularly low: the agency system is expensive to operate (remember that the commission of around 10% is a fair proportion of the normal retailer's margin); bad debts are higher than in a shop

selling on credit; and costs are further increased by the very necessary 'exchange if unsatisfactory' policy that has to be adopted.

A second group of small firms deals in a much narrower range of goods (e.g. garden plants), and these firms operate without agents by obtaining orders either through press advertising or through direct advertising (i.e. sending catalogues to possibly interested persons). Some advertising agencies specialise in selling lists of names and addresses compiled from sources like telephone directories, electoral registers, and so on.

Another group selling a wide variety of miscellaneous goods does so purely by press advertising – look at the 'Market Place' advertisement page of a national newspaper, particularly at the weekend.

It is also worth mentioning that some of the large department stores and at least one variety chain store have in recent years established mail-order departments.

Despite its dynamic growth, mail order still accounts for retail sales of only £1 in every £25.

Automatic vending

This is another area of retailing where, although total annual sales are comparatively low, there have been spectacular increases in the last decade. There may well be nearly half a million machines in operation, selling a range of goods including drinks, sandwiches, chocolate and cigarettes, petrol, books, coal, nylons and tights; machines selling services (e.g. railway tickets and entry to an unmanned car park) must, of course, also be mentioned.

Franchises and leased 'shops'

A franchise is the right to sell the product of a particular process (convenience foods like hamburgers, 'instant' printing, and so on). In return for the tied shops accepting restrictions in trading methods and goods and services sold, the franchise owner grants the operator a monopoly in a specific area as well as other financial and management assistance. It is estimated that total franchise turnover could reach £1 billion in a couple of years.

Leasing floor space involves allocating to a well-known supplier or manufacturer a specific area in a store for selling his products. Basically it is a shop within a shop: the retail store provides various services (telephone, heating and lighting) in return for a commission based on a turnover. This arrangement is very common in department stores.

The changing pattern of retailing

It has already been seen that in the last few decades there have been vast changes in retailing. Some of the causes have been mentioned, but it is useful to summarise them by saying that high labour costs, an increase in branded goods and pre-packaging, improved shop fittings and equipment, an increase in mobility of the customer with less time available for shopping and a generally higher standard of living as a result of – until recently – comparatively full employment, have all favoured the development of the large type of retail organisation. Basically, high street shopping has prospered at the expense of shopping 'round the corner'. The effect of improved technology in products and product-marketing has reduced the need for the knowledgeable retailer; mass-production techniques have meant that it is simpler to exchange units than to repair them; and the division between trades is disappearing as more prepared goods of all descriptions come on the market. The more even distribution of wealth has had far-reaching effects on retailing: department stores provide fewer luxuries for the wealthy; there has been great expansion of multiple shops and chain stores providing good-quality standardised goods and services for the majority; co-operative trading has declined; and, finally, the hire-purchase and credit system of trading has increased enormously, largely because wage earners in regular employment earning good rates of pay can afford regular payments even though they may have little capital.

The economic recession from 1980 onwards, with its great increase in unemployment, has considerably decreased the retail trade's expansion, particularly in the field of 'shopping' goods (the more expensive consumer durables and clothes).

As to the future, the 'automatic' shop is likely to appear soon. Using either an electronic key or a punched card, customers will select goods (possibly at home before the shopping expedition commences) which will be automatically conveyed to a collecting point where the bill, already machine-prepared, will be paid. Telephone orders may also be dealt with by computer equipment.

And in the longer term it is probable that the customer will not have to leave home at all – even the goods themselves may arrive through electronically operated 'pipelines'. Certainly we will move nearer the cashless society – the bank's computer will be able to accept our payment before we leave the hypermarket!

6

Wholesaling

The wholesale function

Basically, the wholesaler is the link between the producer and the retailer or other trader. He buys from the manufacturer or producer in sufficiently large quantities to enable him to resell in smaller batches at a profit. It is important to realise that a considerable proportion of his sales may not be to retailers at all – there are many large organisations, such as hospitals and schools, who will buy direct from the wholesaler.

Our home trade can be classified under two main headings:

1 *Producers' goods* – items needed to satisfy the wants of the consumer indirectly. These include raw materials, components (e.g. speedometers for vehicles) and capital goods (e.g. machinery and equipment).
2 *Consumers' goods*, which can be subdivided into:
   (*a*)   food,
   (*b*)   manufactured goods.

The methods and ways by which goods are distributed vary considerably. For instance, producers' goods are likely to go from the primary producer (e.g. the rubber estate) to the manufacturer or from one manufacturer to another, though in certain circumstances a manufacturer might buy from a wholesaler, particularly if very large quantities were not needed. Consumers' goods will normally be distributed from the manufacturer via possibly one or two intermediaries (wholesalers, brokers and agents) to the retailer.

Bypassing the wholesaler

Obviously the wholesaling costs (including profit) have to be added to the selling price paid by the final consumer. Why not, therefore, shorten the chain of distribution if possible and eliminate the wholesaler? The answer, of course, is that generally producers and manufacturers are free to do so, but the *wholesale function* must still be carried out. Thus the manufacturing firm may have a wholesaling subsidiary and even its own chain of retail shops (an example is Boots the Chemists); large retailers may well have a financial interest in the manufacturer's business; a producer or manufacturer may sell direct to retailers (this happens in the bakery and confectionery trades to some extent, and also in the supply of frozen foods). The wholesaling services still have to be provided by someone; a firm running its own wholesale organisation (e.g. the variety chain stores) can, of course, save the independent wholesaler's profit margin.

Types of wholesaler

It is difficult to classify wholesalers into definite categories because they are so numerous and operate so differently in the many trades. In general terms, however, they can be divided thus:

1 *National wholesalers* covering the whole country. These would be large firms with extensive warehouse facilities.
2 *Area or regional wholesalers or distributors*. They may buy direct from the manufacturer or via a national wholesaler. A good example is in the supply of electrical goods and motor-vehicle accessories.
3 *Local wholesalers*. These, of course, will be smaller than the above two groups. Nowadays, they are likely to be a cash-and-carry firm, particularly if they are dealing with foodstuffs and domestic household goods.
4 *Importers and exporters*. These are dealt with in Chapter 14.

Overall about one million persons are employed in the wholesaling sector, if the term is defined loosely.

The services of the wholesaler

Warehousing (assembly and stockholding)

The wholesaler assembles stocks of goods, generally from different manufacturers; or, in the case of agricultural produce, he may collect small quantities from a large number of producers. Sometimes grading, sorting or prepacking is also involved. Selling through wholesalers gives manufacturers an economic number of large outlets while allowing the retailer to be able to choose the products of a number of rival manufacturers or producers.

The wholesaler will hold reserve stocks (an activity involving both risk and capital) so that he can deal with seasonal demands from the retailer. The wholesaler's job is to attempt to anticipate demand. It makes good sense if the manufacturer can make product X regularly and steadily throughout the year knowing that there are wholesale outlets willing to buy from him and to stock-hold until the goods are needed.

Transfer and delivery

Distribution costs are often very heavy indeed, particularly where the goods are comparatively bulky in relation to their value. Considerable savings can be made in transport expenses as a result of the wholesale function being carried out: consignments can be of economical sizes; the trader can have one delivery of a number of lines at one time. Considerable economies are being effected nowadays by the use of a computerised distribution system, thus enabling both warehouses and vehicles to be used effectively – for example, order of loading and planning of routes can be worked out by computer instead of by rule of thumb.

Expert buying and selling

The wholesaler (or importer or broker) should have the expert knowledge to enable him to buy when prices are low, holding stocks until supplies are less plentiful. This is particularly important in the commodity markets (see Chapter 14), where factors outside human control, such as the weather, may materially affect supplies. Provided that this technique is used reasonably and intelligently, it will help to even out supplies between glut and shortage. Modern methods of storing and preservation have made safe storage easier.

Information

As he is in touch with large numbers of retailers, the wholesaler may be in a position to advise the manufacturer of outlets for his products, of criticism of them, and of the views of retailers about new products needed. However, in recent years, with the development of sophisticated marketing and market-research techniques, the manufacturer has tended to rely on his own intelligence to supply this information.

Finance

The large wholesalers in particular are able to help to finance trade by buying from manufacturers, thus assisting their cash-flow position (which is often precarious because of their heavy capital commitments) and similarly giving long credit terms to small retailers. Obviously the wholesaler ensures that he is recompensed for having his capital 'tied up'. It is important to realise that selling goods on credit is the equivalent of lending money without interest.

Co-operative Wholesale Society

As this is the largest single unit in the wholesale trade in the UK, a special mention is needed. (Co-operative societies as business units are dealt with in Chapter 4 and as retailers in Chapter 5.)

The very name CWS is to some extent a misnomer, as in addition to wholesaling activities it is both manufacturer and producer. Its other interests include tea planting, ship ownership, farming and the operation of more than a hundred factories.

Mention has already been made of the very important part played by the co-operative retail societies. Legal ownership of the Wholesale Society is in the hands of the retail societies themselves; they provide the capital in relation to their size and receive dividends in relation to their purchases. As has already been mentioned, efforts are being made to coordinate more closely the relationship between the wholesale and retail societies.

The other two activities of the CWS that should be mentioned are the Co-operative Bank (which, incidentally, is one of the few banks in this country that pays a small interest on current accounts, see Chapter 9) and the Co-operative Insurance Society – to a very large extent the latter operates quite independently and in many ways resembles the mutual societies (see Chapter 13).

Wholesaling and industry

Most of this chapter has been concerned with consumer goods. Special mention needs to be made, however, of the steel industry, which has employed wholesalers to good effect (as steel stockholders).

Steel manufacturing plants can only operate as large-scale enterprises with long production runs; there are, however, many thousands of comparatively small specialist engineering firms making special orders that require a wide range of metal supplies, often in small quantities. Thus here is a useful activity for the 'middle man'. Some of these firms are very large enterprises – one of these steel stockholders is likely to be holding stocks at various depots of several million pounds in value. It is perhaps not generally realised that around 15% of the number of businesses in the wholesale trade are classified as dealers in 'industrial materials'.

Wholesaling and agriculture

The traditional system for distributing agricultural produce depended on an involved network of local markets and large numbers of middle men. Additionally, in a number of large towns, wholesale produce markets like Covent Garden were established for vegetables, fruits, poultry and flowers. In an industry such as farming, which had tens of thousands of small producers, often in areas with bad communication links to the towns, the advantages of such a wholesale system will be obvious. Wholesalers and agents collected the produce, and often provided technical assistance in matters such as packing and grading.

Since 1931 attempts have been made by successive governments to assist the farmer financially and to encourage the production of more food at home. Under Acts of Parliament, Marketing Boards were set up to organise distribution, to give guaranteed prices to the farmer and to set quality standards. Examples are the Boards which were set up for milk, eggs, potatoes and hops. Although the Marketing Board system is still of importance, generally its influence has declined, particularly since the UK joined the Common Market (see Chapter 14).

Although traditional systems and methods of marketing are still strong, two developments have become increasingly important: farmers in increasing numbers have formed cooperative marketing schemes to reduce their dependence on middle men; and large retail groups (e.g. Marks & Spencer and Sainsbury's) have demonstrated their willingness to take control of both production and distribution, and now advise farmers on growing methods as well as carrying out inspections to ensure that high standards of quality are maintained.

Now that the UK is a full member of the European Economic Community (Chapter 14), further substantial alterations in marketing methods are likely.

The future of the independent wholesaler

It has already been seen that the wholesaling function cannot be eliminated. But it does appear that the importance of the independent wholesaler dealing with consumer goods is likely to diminish still further than it has already done. The big retailers have largely by-passed the wholesaler; and many manufacturers making a higher proportion of branded goods than hitherto prefer to advertise their products themselves and to conduct transactions with retailers direct (it should be remembered that a wholesaler handling several rival manufacturers' goods cannot possibly act in an equitable manner to them all). But it must be borne in mind that direct selling by a manufacturer to a retailer is not administratively cheap, particularly as far as transport and delivery costs are concerned.

There has in recent years been increasing cooperation between wholesalers and the small retailers, and the voluntary group or chain has emerged (already mentioned in Chapter 5). By organised group bulk-buying the small retailers get price advantages, and assistance on matters like shop modernisation is also given. The voluntary chains are now trying to improve the standard of the smaller retailer-member.

One effect of the system is that retailers are being encouraged to reduce the number of competing brands they stock, and in some cases the group or chain has introduced its own branded goods. (Spar, for example, has about 100 privately branded lines.)

The number of 'cash and carry' wholesale warehouses has increased in recent years. By bulk-purchasing and limiting their expenditure on premises, credit and delivery facilities, they can offer large price discounts to their customers. It is estimated that by 1980 there were 600 'cash and carry' depots in Britain.

7

Terms of Sale

A typical business transaction on credit

The buying of goods (or services) is in law a binding contract. A pays, or agrees to pay, a certain sum of money for certain goods or services provided on certain terms, or to be provided, by B. Technically, one party makes an 'offer', the other party 'accepts' and 'consideration' is given. Most contracts can be oral, but it is obviously better if certain details are committed to paper. Remember that there is a valid contract as soon as agreement has been reached – the fact that goods have not been delivered or money paid makes no difference. It is therefore vital to ensure that at the moment a legal contract exists both parties are quite clear about their obligations.

1 The inquiry

If goods are being ordered from a priced catalogue, then this step can normally be dispensed with – in this case, the transaction begins at (3) (see page 69).

The business firm wishing to order goods is likely to get in touch with several potential suppliers; he will have obtained their names from trade directories or journals, classified telephone directories (Yellow Pages), trade associations, chambers of commerce or possibly from a business acquaintance in the same trade. Either a printed form would be used or an ordinary typed letter would be sent by the inquirer.

2 The quotation

This is the 'offer' referred to above. It should contain not only the quantities that can be supplied and the price, but also information about delivery dates, method of delivery and payment terms. For standard goods it may only be necessary to send a catalogue and price list, but in a large number of cases a specially prepared quotation will become necessary. A typical quotation might be as follows:

(Note that VAT (Value Added Tax) details will normally have to be given on quotations and invoices, but for simplicity these are omitted in the documents in this chapter. VAT is dealt with on page 77.)

QUOTATION   No. 931 X

The Westbrook Manufacturing Company Limited
Whiteheath
LONDON SE3 0NP

Tel: 01-990 9999

17 March 198–

Christopher and Susan Abbott & Co.
Chartered Architects
The Mound
LINCOLN

In reply to your inquiry dated 8 March 198– under reference PG/ZP, we are pleased to advise that we can supply goods as follows:

Quantity	Ref. No.	Description	Gross Price
6	ZC 164	Walnut Single Right-hand Pedestal Desks 2.00 m × 1.00 m	£51.35 each

(as attached illustration)

Delivery:	One month from receipt of your order.
Terms:	Trade discount 25%,[1] carriage paid[2] to your works.
Payment:	Cash discount 2%[3] for settlement within 10 days of invoice date or net monthly (payment due 15th of month following delivery date).

(Signed) R. P. Nosraw, Sales Manager

Notes
[1]Trade discount – the price quoted is subject to a 25% discount. Many firms quote this way; it enables them to show a gross price in their printed advertising literature, and they can vary the discount according to quantity purchased. This practice is particularly common in transactions between wholesalers and retailers.

[2]Carriage paid – the seller will arrange transport for the goods and will bear the cost himself. Other common terms are:

Carriage forward – the buyer is charged an additional sum for transport costs.

Ex works or ⎫ – the buyer will have to arrange his own transport and
Ex factory ⎭ collect the goods from the seller's premises.

[3]The goods are being sold on *credit* terms. The buyer has the choice of paying the full sum on a monthly account basis or settling within ten days in return for a 2% discount. Some suppliers give limited credit to a new customer before making inquiries as to his credit standing. Others insist on cash-with-order terms for a first order (particularly if the buyer is not known to them). Many suppliers are subscribers to a firm of mercantile inquiry agents – for example, Dun & Bradstreet, who supply reports on the financial status of prospective buyers. Suppliers with a large number of credit accounts find it worthwhile to pay an annual subscription to one of these agencies, thus obtaining annually its credit ratings register – five volumes listing, geographically, brief details about the majority of businesses in the country (excluding small-scale retailers). Additionally, or alternatively, trade or bank references are requested from the potential buyer (note that, in the case of a banker's reference, application must be made by the creditor to his own bankers, who will pass the inquiry on to the buyer's banker).

3 The order
Having received several quotations, the buyer will make his decision. It does not follow that he will choose the cheapest quotation; he will take the other factors already referred to into account. For example, X may be charging a little more but offers a better delivery date or more generous credit terms. The buyer will then send out his firm order (this legally is the 'acceptance' – both parties now have obligations), which might look like this:

ORDER	No. 83

Christopher and Susan Abbott & Co.
Chartered Architects
The Mound, Lincoln

Tel: Lincoln 9990
(STD code 0522)[1]   23 March 198–

The Westbrook Manufacturing Co. Ltd
Whiteheath
LONDON SE3 0NP

Your Quotation No. 931 X dated 17 March 198–[2]

Please supply:

6 Walnut Single Right-hand Pedestal Desks at £51.35 each less 25%
trade discount, carriage paid to our works.[3]

C. J. R. Abbott

Notes
[1]STD – Subscriber Trunk Dialling (see Chapter 10).
[2]It is obviously helpful if each party quotes the other's reference number.
[3]The buyer will be obliged to conform to the terms of sale even though he
has not repeated them fully on the order. If he had any objections he would
have to raise them before placing a firm order.

4   Dealing with the order

Each seller will have his own system for processing the order. Many
will use labour-saving mechanised means to produce the documents
required. A medium-sized sales department might produce the
paperwork on accounting machines, using electrically operated
calculators for the arithmetical work needed. Many firms nowadays
are very likely to use a wholly computerised system in which the
only semi-manual operation is likely to be the punching of the card,
tape or disc with details of the sale. Even a quite small firm using the
typewriter may use *continuous stationery* (specially prepared sets of
documents in a continuous roll or *concertina*), using a sensitised
paper which eliminates the need for carbon paper and which, with
the aid of a small metal frame added to the typewriter, obviates the
need for the typist to remove each document after it is typed.

The order may be automatically acknowledged, though businesses supplying from stock may eliminate this step. When the goods are ready for despatch the major documentation takes place. Sometimes an advice note is sent, advising the buyer that the goods are about to be despatched, although again this may well be omitted if time in transit is short. A delivery note invariably accompanies the goods, and the bill or invoice is generally sent by post separately. As the advice/delivery notes contain much of the information that has to be included on the invoice, they can often be prepared simultaneously by machine. There may well be several copies of the invoice, sometimes in different colours – the top copy goes to the buyer, one copy is used for the seller's own book-keeping purposes, another may be passed to the sales representative, and so on. The set of documents can be so designed that certain portions of information will only appear on any specific copy; for example, many firms prefer that the despatch department is not given the prices.

DELIVERY NOTE   No. A 734

The Westbrook Manufacturing Company Limited
Whiteheath
LONDON SE3 0NP

Tel: 01-990 9999

1 April 198–

Christopher and Susan Abbott & Co.
Chartered Architects
The Mound
LINCOLN

Your Order 83 dated 23 March

Please receive the following in good order:

Description	Quantity	Packages
Walnut Single Right-hand Pedestal Desks	6	6

Very often two copies of the delivery note are sent, one being signed by the buyer's receiving department. Rarely is it possible to examine the goods in detail; the most that can normally be done is to ensure that the correct number of packages are received and that there is no obvious external damage. Sellers usually make some sort of stipulation that damaged or incorrect goods must be returned within a limited time.

INVOICE   No. B 734[1]

The Westbrook Manufacturing Company Limited
Whiteheath
LONDON SE3 0NP

Tel: 01-990 9999

1 April 198–

Christopher and Susan Abbott & Co.
Chartered Architects
The Mound
LINCOLN

Your Order 83 dated 23 March – our Delivery Note A 734 1 April

Description	*Quantity*	*Unit Price* £	*Amount* £
Walnut Single Right-hand Pedestal Desks	6	51.35	308.10
Less 25% Trade Discount			77.03
Net due			231.07[2]

Payment terms:

  2% cash discount for settlement by 11 April, or
  Net monthly (payment due 15 May).[3]

Notes

[1]B 734 – Invoice bears same number as delivery note since it has been prepared as part of a preprinted set but bears a different prefix for easy identification.

[2]As already mentioned, VAT has not been included (see below).

[3]Monthly settlement does not normally mean payment to be received exactly one month after invoice date. In practice, some regular arrangement is made (in this case in the middle of the next month).

5 Dealing with the invoice

The seller will make the appropriate book-keeping entries to record that a sale has been made and that he is owed money – although the necessary accounting is outside the scope of this book (interested readers should refer to *Book-keeping* by D. Cousins, published by Teach Yourself Books), a simple ledger account is shown below. Readers will realise from this that every time the customer is charged a sum of money he is debited and whenever money is received from the customer he is credited; similarly, whenever it is necessary to reduce the original charge (e.g. if he returns faulty goods) he is credited.

The buyer for his part has to satisfy himself that (i) he has received the goods as ordered, (ii) the correct price has been charged and (iii) the correct discounts have been given. Many systems are in existence for doing this. For example, the receiving department check and initial the delivery note confirming (i); this is passed to the buying department so that they can match up this document with the invoice, themselves checking prices and discounts from their copy of the order thus satisfactorily dealing with (ii); the purchase accounts department then complete the operation by checking the calculations and making the entry in the supplier's account. It is their job to ensure that payment is made in time to earn the discount, which they obtain by paying 2p per £ less than the sum charged. If the buyer is not satisfied with the goods (and this may arise because they are not exactly as ordered, or are damaged, or there has been a short delivery) he will advise the seller and return the goods where appropriate. Very often the invoice may have been passed for payment before the fault is discovered (for example, extensive laboratory tests may be needed); in this case, assuming the seller agrees to reduce the invoice charge and sends a credit note (the opposite of an invoice), the buyer will pass the credit note through his books. A credit note is often printed in red and would read as follows:

CREDIT NOTE   No. X 16

6 April

Our Invoice B 734 1 April
Your letter dated 4 April, reference 83/R/GKB[1]

We have credited your account as follows:

1 Walnut Single Right-hand Pedestal Desk returned as
   damaged   £38.51[2]

Replacement will be sent in 10 days and charged separately.[3]

Notes
[1]The buyer had used a reference comprising these elements (his letter is not illustrated):

        83 – his original order number.
        R – indicating 'returned'.
        GKB – initials of responsible member of staff.

[2]The seller did *not* charge £51.35 per desk but allowed 25% reduction.
[3]Most sellers follow this practice; it avoids the difficulties that arise if replacements have to be sent out free of charge.

6 The ledger account

The above transaction would be recorded in a personal account for the buyer as already explained. At any one time the buyer owes the excess of the debits over the credits. A simple but satisfactory explanation is that the buyer is in debt to the extent of the total debits less the total credits (or amounts in his favour). A ledger account that might be prepared by a book-keeping machine is shown below.

Customer: Christopher and Susan Abbott & Co.

Credit limit £1000[1]

Date	Details	Debits £	Credits £	Balance[2] £
April 1	Invoice B 734	231.07		231.07
April 6	Credit note X 16		38.51	192.56
April 10	Cheque		188.71	
	Discount		3.85	NIL

Notes

[1]Credit control was referred to on page 69. As a result of their inquiries, the seller is willing to allow the customer up to £1000 credit at any one time. He will not normally disclose this figure to the customer and, in the light of the way the account is conducted and orders received, he may adjust it. If unwilling to grant credit, the seller will normally sell on a *cash with order* (CWO) or *proforma invoice* basis; that is, when the goods are ready for despatch the buyer is asked to pay and the consignment is then sent.

[2]Any accounting machine or computer is capable of doing the necessary arithmetic. This column shows the amount outstanding at any one time.

[3]The buyer having returned one desk owes for only five of them. As he has paid within the stipulated period, he deducts 2p in the £ from £192.56 and pays the remainder, thus clearing the account. Fractions of pence are, of course, ignored in calculations. If he had another delivery of goods before the 10 April, then the necessary charge would have been entered. Thus, if it is assumed that he had bought another £100 worth on 8 April and had then paid for the first consignment in the same way, this ledger account would have appeared thus:

		Debits £	*Credits* £	*Balance* £
same details as above up to this point				192.56
April 8	Invoice B 742	100.00		292.56
April 10	Cheque		188.71	
	Discount		3.85	100.00

7   Statement of account

Normally the creditor (the person to whom money is owed) sends the debtor a statement at regular intervals, usually monthly, setting out the month's transactions, commencing with any sum owing at the beginning and ending with the final sum due at the end of the month. The statement and invoice contain a great deal of common information and therefore can be prepared simultaneously by book-keeping machine or similar system. It would be an exact duplicate of the ledger account but would omit the credit limit and would be likely to have printed at the bottom

    Settlement due by _____.

Some firms prepare statements by photocopying the ledger accounts on a high-speed electrostatic copier (e.g. Rank Xerox). In this case, credit limit would not appear on the ledger account; a different system of recording this would be used. Computer users are able to produce statements automatically. Increasingly accounting is being carried out by computer methods.

8   Payment of accounts and receipts
Methods of payment in use are:

Cash. Some retailers still settle their accounts by cash, particularly in cases where a representative calls regularly. Legal tender (i.e. cash that must be accepted) consists of:

Notes and £1 coin – no maximum; 50p coins – up to £10; 5p, 10p and 20p coins – up to £5; 2p coins and below – up to 20p.

Post Office remittance service (postal orders). Businesses rarely settle bills in this way, though it is used extensively in mail order (see Chapter 5).

National Girobank. This is dealt with in Chapter 10. It is a very suitable method for payment if both parties have Giro accounts as no charge is made.

Cheques or *credit transfers* (commercial banks). The vast majority of business debts are settled this way. In certain circumstances direct debits are suitable (see Chapter 9).

Bills of exchange. Normally used only in connection with foreign trade (see Chapter 8).

Whichever payment method is used, it is vital to advise the creditor how the amount is arrived at. There are various ways of doing this: some firms return the statement they have received duly amended if necessary; others use a remittance advice, which is a document setting out the total being paid and showing the individual items.

At one time it was standard practice to send receipts, but over the years the practice has grown up in many firms of saving clerical costs by not sending receipts for cheque payments unless specially requested by the debtor, and often the statement sent out by the creditor contains this information. The reason why the receipt can so often be omitted is that, for any payment through the banking or giro system, evidence of payment can be obtained if necessary from the bank; the item appears on the bank statement, and although most banks do not automatically nowadays return paid cheques to their customers, they are available in the event of a query. Receipts are, of course, important where payment is made in cash.

Value Added Tax (VAT)

As part of the plan to eventually introduce a standard system of indirect taxation in the Common Market countries (Chapter 14), Value Added Tax came into effect on 1 April 1973 and replaced both Purchase Tax and Selective Employment Tax. Purchase Tax had been charged from 1944 on a wide range of mainly consumer goods at a variety of rates depending on the 'luxury' element of the items; there were a number of exemptions (e.g. food, fuel). Administratively, it was cheap and easy to collect, as the authorities had to deal only with manufacturers and wholesalers. Selective Employment Tax was paid on the number of employees but generally applied only to the service trades and construction industry.

VAT, unlike Purchase Tax, is collected in instalments, in the sense that liability to tax arises on the 'value added' at each stage in the productive and distribution processes. Imports are not exempt, and tax is also levied on the supply of services (e.g. hotel bills, car hire, tickets for entertainments). The original rate was 10%,[1] and two categories not charged to tax were introduced:

1. Exempt – examples are banking and insurance, postal, education and health services.
2. Zero rating – examples are food, books and newspapers, children's clothing, transport services and all exports.

A zero-rated concern is in a more favourable category than an exempt one because, although neither charges tax on its sales, the former can reclaim the tax it itself has paid on its purchases (thus an exporter who pays tax on a calculator he has bought can recover the tax, but a bank cannot).

---

[1]There have been several changes since then and the current rate (1983) is 15%. As VAT can be used as an economic regulator, the rate is likely to change from time to time.

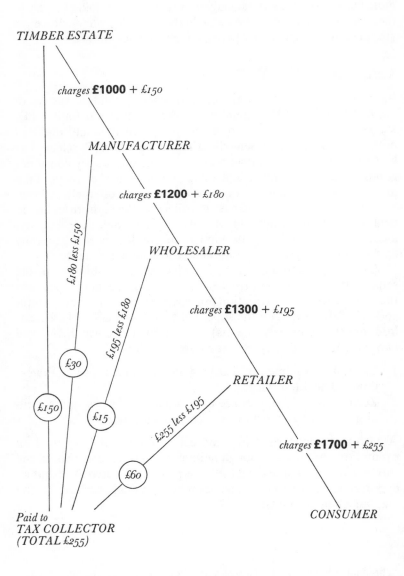

TIMBER ESTATE

charges **£1000** + *£150*

MANUFACTURER

charges **£1200** + *£180*

WHOLESALER

charges **£1300** + *£195*

RETAILER

charges **£1700** + *£255*

£180 less £150

£195 less £180

£255 less £195

£30

£150

£15

£60

Paid to
TAX COLLECTOR
(TOTAL £255)

CONSUMER

VAT calculated at standard rate of 15%. The sums in bold type represent the
basic selling prices required by each trader.

Collection of VAT

VAT is a consumer tax, for it is the ultimate buyer who finally pays the tax on the purchase price. Broadly speaking, all traders in the UK with annual turnovers in excess of £5000 (this figure has since been increased to £15000) became tax collectors on 1 April, 1973 – they pay to the Customs and Excise Department every three months an amount equal to the tax they have charged their customers (output) less the tax they themselves have suffered (input). The invoice on page 72 will have had a 15% tax addition calculated on the gross price less trade and cash discounts (regardless of whether the buyer takes advantage of the cash-discount terms).

The diagram on page 78 shows a simplified example of the charging and collection system through the production and distribution processes. In practice, settlement with the tax authorities is made in bulk and there would be many other items for services and so on. VAT is a complicated tax to operate and collection costs are higher than with Purchase Tax. The Customs and Excise Department have to have dealings with several hundred thousand business firms, many of whom will be dealing with chargeable, zero-rated and exempt categories. Finally, it should be mentioned that small traders (under £15000 yearly turnover referred to above) are exempt from VAT and do not need to register or keep VAT records. But their customers will still pay tax on purchases, for the small trader will himself pay tax as appropriate when he buys goods and services, and will pass this on. Normally, retailers do not show the VAT amount separately when indicating prices, though will issue a detailed VAT invoice if requested.

8

Money and Banking

How and why banks began

If our ancestors wished to obtain goods and services they used the barter system – offering other goods or services in exchange. This was obviously difficult and inconvenient; how much corn was equal to a pig, and suppose you did not want a whole animal? Gradually it was realised that some acceptable common commodity was needed as a medium of exchange. Many were tried (cowrie shells were used extensively in South-east Asia) and discarded. Ideally, the 'money-thing' needed to be relatively scarce and thus valuable (so earth – except in a desert – was unsuitable); light and compact (so elephant tusks – used in some communities – were not satisfactory); and durable so that it did not lose value (thus salt – though often scarce – would not be acceptable). The commodities that eventually found favour proved to be precious stones and rare minerals like gold and silver. Eventually gold and silver became the generally accepted currency; they could easily be shaped into manageable small pieces of varying weights and value – hence the coin. By the seventeenth century gold and silver coins were in general use in Europe for trading purposes.

In early societies coins were worth what they weighed. If by weight they were worth more than their face value, then they would be melted down. If, as often happened, their face value was in excess of their weight value, they were normally not acceptable. There always was a temptation to 'clip' coins despite severe penalties, and on a number of occasions recoinage has been necessary to correct debasement. It was the invention of the milled edge that eventually provided a check on simple clipping. Nowadays, we use token coins made of cupro nickel or bronze. They are worth more as coins than as metals.

The first paper money (again, token money) was the bank note introduced by the early goldsmiths. Their vaults were used by wealthy persons to keep their valuables and surplus gold coins, for which receipts were issued and surrendered when coins were withdrawn. The coins taken back from the goldsmith were often used to pay debts to persons who themselves deposited the gold in return for a further receipt. It can therefore be seen how a system evolved whereby the receipts were transferred, thus avoiding moving the gold. The goldsmiths later began to issue notes for fixed amounts instead of receipts for varying amounts. These notes were payable to bearer (i.e. to the holder) instead of, as with the first receipts, to a named person. Thus formal bank notes came into being.

The next development was that goldsmiths allowed their customers to issue letters of instruction to them to pay a fixed amount to someone else – and so the modern cheque!

The introduction of the above methods of payment meant that there was less actual movement of gold, and so the goldsmiths began to build up a surplus in excess of the normal requirements of their customers. They therefore began to lend a part of it to other merchants in need of temporary finance – and thus goldsmiths became our first lending bankers.

It was seen above that paper money has no intrinsic value. In the last resort its worth depended on the honesty and integrity of the banker. Did he actually have gold to back his notes? If a financial crisis arose (and these were even more common than now) in a fast-growing economy and there was a 'run' on the bank, then if the banker did not have enough gold to meet demands the holders of notes stood to lose their money.

Eventually the Bank of England (see page 83) took over the note issue in the middle of the last century, though this process was not completed until 1921. The Bank of England held gold to back most of the notes in issue until 1919. Successive world financial crises led to a general realisation that this system had major deficiencies, and the gold standard was finally abandoned in 1931, since which date it is the credit of the government that is relied on; for the promise to pay the bearer £x that appears on every note is honoured by giving another promise on another bank note (we call this the *fiduciary issue* – the notes issued are backed by government securities). When a country's credit fails (as in Germany in 1918 and 1945) the currency collapses and barter or semi-barter takes its place – cigarettes were used in a number of European countries both in and after the Second World War.

Bills of exchange and credit

The cheque (as mentioned above, originally the customer's letter to his goldsmith-banker) has long since replaced coins and notes for most of our commercial transactions. But the cheque is a form of *bill of exchange*, which for centuries has been a way in which a trader could transfer the ownership (the title) of goods and services to another party without using currency. Although its modern use is largely restricted to some foreign trade transactions (Chapter 14) and dealings between the financial institutions and the authorities (see page 88), nevertheless it is important to understand its use as a replacement for money. The following is an illustration of a bill of exchange.

£10 000	Canberra 1 January, 198–

Three months after date pay to our order the sum of £10 000 sterling for value received.

| To: J. Smith,
　　London SW1. | (Signed) K. McGowran |

Here the drawer (K. McGowran) is instructing J. Smith to pay him £10 000 in three months' time for goods bought by the latter. This is a valueless piece of paper until it is 'accepted' by the party to whom it is addressed. This would be done thus:

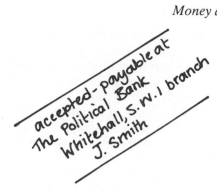

accepted - payable at
The Political Bank
Whitehall, S.W.1 branch
J. Smith

In the above case, K. McGowran is both the drawer and the payee. He could have required the money to be paid to a third party:

> ... pay to Mr R. Carr the sum ...

McGowran can either wait for three months (plus three days of grace) and pay the bill into his bank for collection in the normal way, or 'sell' it to a financial institution (who would charge him a discount for immediate cash), or transfer it to someone else to whom he himself owed money and who was prepared to accept it. Obviously the bill depends on Smith's credit-worthiness for its negotiability value.

The use of the cheque (or the credit transfer, direct debit or credit card, all referred to in the next chapter) have reduced dependence on actual cash, although vast amounts of the latter are still needed. In an average month the notes and coins in circulation total over £10 000 million, but the value of cheques passing through the bankers' clearing house (Chapter 9) in 1980 was nearly £4 500 000 million and the volume of bank deposits in the UK is five or six times the volume of notes issued. The most important form of money is now bank deposit money. What changes hands is not cash but the right to cash.

The Bank of England and the money market

Some mention has already been made of this institution. Founded in 1694 to raise money for the military junketings abroad of William III and to provide a better banking service than the goldsmiths could, it gradually acquired one of its major functions, that of being the 'bankers' bank' – that is, the commercial banks kept their surplus funds with the Bank of England. Because of recurring financial crises at the beginning of the nineteenth century, the Bank gradually acquired special powers and responsibilities (the sole issue of bank notes has already been referred to) and became a central bank. Although it remained a profit-making joint-stock company, it became the government's agency responsible for carrying out its monetary policy. There was criticism, particularly during the 1930s, that it often put its own financial interests before those of the nation. The first post-war Labour government national-ised the Bank of England in 1946 (see Chapter 4), the shareholders receiving government stock as compensation. Its directors are now appointed by the government, which has legal power to issue directions to the Bank. Its duties and responsibilities can be summa-rised as follows:

1   To control the note issue. As already mentioned, the majority of the issue is backed by securities (other bits of paper), not gold. The amount not backed by gold is called the fiduciary issue (from a Latin term meaning trust). It is varied from time to time to meet the demand of the public for cash (for example at Christmas or at summer holiday periods).

2   To act as the bankers' bank (this has already been referred to). The commercial banks maintain current accounts with the Bank of England and each bank uses these balances to settle trans-actions with other banks (see page 95). Below the reader will see how the Bank can control these balances by dealing in securities.

3   To act as the government's banker, to advise them on monetary policy and to manage the national debt (that is, sums invested by the public in government stocks, bonds, certificates, and so on; plus amounts owing to foreign countries, mainly to the USA and Canada). A high proportion of the debt has been incurred in waging two world wars. The Bank can influence monetary conditions by its dealings with discount houses (see below). If the Bank wishes to withdraw cash from the banking system it sells government securities in the 'open market', thus transfer-ring funds from the public to the Bank. Bank deposits reduce and the banks may then need to call in loans and advances.

Conversely, if the Bank wishes to increase bank liquidity in an attempt to increase spending, it will itself buy securities. Many economists feel that the tasks listed in this section are amongst the most important functions of the Bank.

4 To be the 'lender of last resort' to City financial institutions (see *The discount houses* below). Until 1981 interest varied with the minimum lending rate fixed by the Bank in conjunction with the Treasury. The Bank no longer announces continually the rate at which it will lend, though it continues to be 'lender of last resort'.

5 To operate the exchange equalisation account. This consists of buying and selling sterling in the money market in an attempt to keep its value steady in terms of other currencies. If there is an adverse balance of payments (see Chapter 14), there will be pressure on the £ sterling and the Bank may have to use its precious gold and dollar reserves to buy sterling in an attempt to ease the situation.

The discount houses

These institutions specialise in discounting bills of exchange (page 82). They obtain funds by borrowing mainly from the commercial banks at a marginally lower rate of interest than they charge for discounting bills. A high proportion of these are short-term Treasury bills, which is the way the government raises its short-term finance. These bills may well change hands several times before they mature, as commercial banks, industrial companies, pension funds, and so on with money to spare may 'buy' them from the discount houses. If the discount houses are themselves short of funds (because the commercial banks have no surplus funds to lend them), then the Bank of England will themselves either buy Treasury bills from the discount houses or, on occasion, will lend them money at an appropriate rate referred to above. The reader may well think that the discount house is merely an unnecessary intermediary in financial transactions; however, its members are experienced and established financial experts whose know-how is of inestimable value in the money market. The discount houses accept as a formal responsibility that they should cover the government's need to borrow on Treasury bills offered on tender each week.

The accepting houses

These again are specialist financial institutions (many are old-established merchant bankers). Reference has been made to the importance of being able to establish the credit standing of the acceptor of a bill of exchange. The accepting house, as a result of the 'intelligence' provided by their network of agents throughout the world, are able to make a very accurate assessment of a firm's status and in appropriate cases will 'lend their name' or 'accept' a bill in return for a small commission of perhaps 1½%. The bill thus acquires first-class standing and will be able to be discounted without trouble.

Merchant banks

Names such as Rothschild, Baring and Lazard may be known to readers. It is financial houses such as these that established themselves in the UK almost 200 years ago and have since undertaken a wide range of business activities. Some are discounting and accepting houses, and many specialise in arranging large loans here for Commonwealth and foreign countries or act as advisers to large businesses, particularly in connection with the raising of finance. Reference was made in Chapter 2 to the raising of capital by joint-stock companies, and merchant bankers often act as issuing houses, dealing with the issuing of stocks and shares. It is their expertise, something gathered over centuries, and their knowledge and experience of foreign trade that enables them to be able to carry out such a wide variety of financial functions.

Finance houses

These businesses (originally called industrial banks) initially specialised in providing finance for hire-purchase transactions. In recent years many have extended their activities and lend much more generally than hitherto (second mortgages, personal loans, etc.). Names like United Dominions Trust Ltd will be known to many. A number of these finance houses are now connected with the joint-stock banks. To attract deposits they offer higher rates of interest than the latter and therefore need to charge borrowers correspondingly more. They perform a very useful function in making finance available in a wide variety of instances where it would not be possible to raise money through normal banking channels.

9

The Commercial Banks

The functions of a commercial bank

A commercial bank has four main functions:

1 To accept from its customers the deposit of money (current, deposit and savings accounts).
2 To collect and transfer money both at home and abroad.
3 To lend money to its customers.
4 To undertake the actual physical distribution of notes and coin throughout the country.

   It also provides a wide range of additional services, which are referred to later in this chapter. Readers who wish to know more about banks and banking are recommended to read *Banking* in the Teach Yourself Books series.

Current accounts

The main service provided by a bank for its customers is facilities through this type of account whereby funds can be:

(*a*)   Added to (deposited in) an account either by the customer himself or by another party.
(*b*)   Withdrawn by the customer himself or by another party authorised by him.
(*c*)   Transferred to another party's current account at any bank (by accounting entry).

   These facilities and the relevant documents used are considered below in more detail. It will, of course, be realised that, although the bank is often called the *custodian* of moneys deposited by customers, it does not undertake to repay the *actual money* deposited – the banker is free to use his customer's money in the most profitable way possible (see page 99).

Many customers use a bank purely for the current-account service and rarely, if ever, use any of the other facilities referred to later in this chapter. The real value of the current account is that, owing to the existence of the clearing house system (see page 95), any bank will *collect* or *pay* money value from or to any other bank.

Opening a current account requires little formality. A reference may be needed to confirm the prospective customer's bona fide status. Several specimen signatures will be required – for generally the bank will be liable if it pays out against a forged cheque; in the case of accounts in the name of firms or organisations, nominated persons sign on behalf of the body concerned. There is no fixed minimum deposit and there is no objection to minors (under 18 years of age) holding accounts. As the clerical costs of maintaining current accounts are high, banks may make a charge for the privilege of having an account; the various banks assess these charges in a variety of ways, but basically they depend on the number of debit accounting entries necessary on the customer's account and the average or minimum balance kept in the account. As a rough guide at the present time (1983) no charge is likely to be made if a balance of £100 is kept in the account, but changes are likely to occur from time to time depending on the banks' profitability records. Bank managers have considerable discretion in this matter of calculating charges; a business firm often makes special arrangements with its bank which result in concessions being given to employees who use the same bank and whose salaries are paid through the credit-transfer system (see page 97).

Paying in to the bank
Using the special paying-in slip provided (or a credit-transfer slip if another branch or bank is used), cash, cheques, postal orders and other forms of 'representative' money can be deposited into the current account. If the customer uses his own branch, then the necessary credit entry will be made in his account more quickly than if he pays in at another bank – although since computerisation has been introduced, the time delay has been reduced.

Payments by cheque

A cheque is a written instruction to the bank where the account is held to pay a certain sum of money *on demand* to the named payee. It is legally a bill of exchange (see page 82). A specimen cheque is shown below, together with explanatory notes.

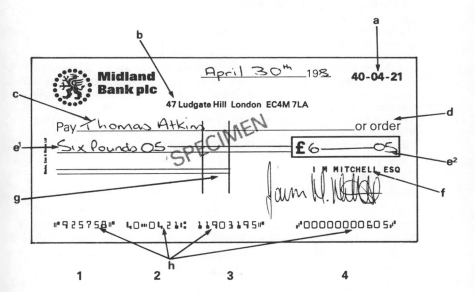

Notes

(*a*) The branch/bank identification code number – all cheques drawn on this particular branch office bear this number.

(*b*) The drawee – the branch where the account holder maintains his account.

(*c*) The payee – if the account holder is withdrawing cash, it is usual to insert the one word 'Cash'.

(*d*) Virtually all cheques are made payable 'or order' (see explanation below under negotiation of cheques). A cheque could be made payable 'or bearer', which means that whoever presents it for payment is entitled to the amount stated, but in view of the risks involved this style is rare.

(e^1) and (e^2). If the cheque is hand-written a hyphen is used; if typed or printed a decimal point is made. Note that if a cheque is for an amount under £1 it should be made out thus:

Words: Sixty eight pence ——————————————————
Figures: £0-68

Care should always be taken to ensure, by using dashes and not leaving spaces, that alterations cannot be made. For example, £6 has been easily altered in the following case:

| Six | pounds | £6 |
| Sixty | pounds | £60-00 |

(*f*) The drawer – the account holder.
(*g*) The crossing – see notes below.
(*h*) Magnetic ink character recognition (MICR) – this gets information relating to the branch book-keeping into the computer. (1), (2) and (3) represent the cheque number, the bank/branch number referred to in (*a*) and the customer's account number respectively; these are already printed on the cheque when the customer receives his cheque book. (4) is a transaction code, identifying the type of voucher being processed, and the amount of the cheque; this is printed on during the clearing process. Readers interested in the application of computer processes to banking should obtain a free booklet *Banks and Automation* from the Bank Education Service, 10 Lombard Street, London EC3.

Cashing of cheques

A cheque that is *open* (i.e. does not have the two parallel lines drawn across the face of the cheque as shown above, or has had the crossing cancelled by the account holder as shown on page 93) can be presented at the bank *on which it is drawn* and exchanged for cash over the counter; unless special arrangements have been made, it cannot be taken to another branch. The account holder (in the cheque illustrated, Thomas Atkins) will be able to withdraw cash up to a certain maximum (at present £50) at other branches of his own bank (or, under some circumstances, at other banks) on presentation of an acceptable cheque card or credit card (see page 104). The reason for this restriction on cash withdrawal is that the branch where the account is held is the only one that knows the credit balance in hand.

With increasing mechanisation it is expected that eventually it will be a simple matter for any branch to check the balance on an account held at another branch; this, of course, will improve cheque-cashing facilities. Increasingly, banks are providing *cash dispensers* at branches for creditworthy customers, who are given a special card or vouchers to use this facility. Recently, several banks have introduced a more sophisticated dispenser linked direct to the computer; this will authorise or reject the customer's request for a named sum keyed by him: it will also provide an up-to-date statement of account and accept deposits.

Crossed cheques

There is not a great deal of security value in an open cheque, any more than there is in an open postal order (see Chapter 10). Anyone finding or stealing it is likely to have little trouble cashing it at the branch on which it is drawn, since all he has to do is to endorse the cheque using the name of the payee; it is not part of the bank's duty to check identity, nor would this be a reliable safeguard. Most cheques are therefore *crossed* (see below), because with such a cheque cash will *not* be paid over the counter under any circumstances. The money value is 'collected' by the bank where the cheque is deposited (see page 95), the necessary transfer being effected by accounting entries only, without any cash actually being physically paid over. If therefore a crossed cheque falls into the wrong hands, the paying bank (in our example, Midland) can be instructed to refuse payment if the loss is discovered in time; if it is too late to do this, there will be a record of whose account the cheque was paid into. Appropriate action can then be taken to recover the money wrongly paid.

There are two types of crossing:

1 *General crossing.* This is the one commonly used. Often the words '& Co.' are added, but this has no particular significance, merely being a relic of early banking practice. A cheque with a general crossing can be paid into *any* bank and normally can be paid into another person's account (see later).

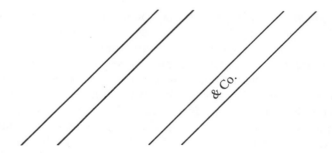

2 *Special crossing.* This is an added precaution, because it ensures that the cheque can be paid only into a particular bank and sometimes to a named account only. A few examples are:

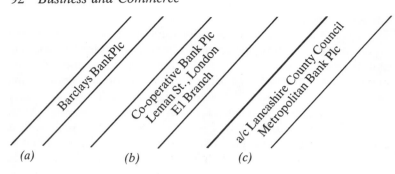

(a)   (b)   (c)

(a)   Cheque can be paid into any Barclays branch.
(b)   Although the drawer has named a particular branch, the cheque can nevertheless be paid in to any branch of the Co-operative Bank.
(c)   Cheque can only be paid into the named account at the bank referred to.

In practice, the vast majority of cheques have a general, and not a special crossing; for normal purposes, the former precaution is sufficient. However, some account holders sometimes add one or both of the following:

Account payee. This is an instruction that the cheque should be paid only into the account of the payee stated and not passed on to another person.

Not negotiable. This makes a cheque doubly safe. Legally, a cheque resembles a pound note in that it is a negotiable instrument; that is, whoever acquires it properly becomes the true owner – so if I steal a note and use it for a purchase in a shop, the shopkeeper is entitled to keep it. Under certain circumstances, therefore, a 'good' cheque drawn by X payable to A could be acquired by B irregularly yet subsequently be used properly and handed to C; C would become the legal owner and A might be in a position to demand payment from X. To protect himself, therefore, X could mark his cheques 'not negotiable'. This does not prevent it being passed on to another person but ensures that anyone who accepts it can have no greater right to it than any previous holder; thus in the above case, C will not be entitled to the money because B (a previous holder) had no right to it. In practice, of course, C is likely to be unwilling to take a 'not negotiable' cheque unless he knows B personally.

Negotiation of cheques
A cheque payable to '———— or bearer' can be passed on without any formality. Owing to risk of loss, almost all cheques are payable to '———— or order'. To transfer an order cheque to another person (say, A. Brown) the payee (say, B. Morley) should either

(a) sign his name on the back of the cheque, or
(b) write 'Pay A. Brown or order' followed by his signature; this is called a special endorsement.

In theory, there is no limit to the number of times a cheque can be so endorsed. In practice, however, the number of cheques endorsed even once is very small – one case when this occurs is when a person without a bank account asks someone to cash his cheque; the latter individual (possibly a shopkeeper) will then pay it into his own account for collection.

Cancellation of a crossing
As has been seen, the crossing is a precaution to protect the account holder. It therefore follows that only the account holder can cancel a crossing. The need for this arises because banks prefer only to issue books of cheques (generally containing thirty cheques) which already have a printed crossing on them. As previously mentioned, this sort of cheque cannot be cashed over the bank counter, so if the account holder wants to allow a payee, known to his bank, to draw cash, he cancels the crossing thus:

The paying bank may well cash such a cheque for a small amount made out to a payee unknown to them on production of suitable proof of identity.

Precautions in the use of cheques

The commercial banks issue the following recommendations to their customers:

1 Use the printed order form in the cheque book when requesting a new cheque book.
2 Write in ink, leaving no spaces for other words or figures to be inserted (business firms often print the information by mechanised means, e.g. computer).
3 Sign your name (not just your initials) against any alteration – in practice, it is best not to alter cheques at all.
4 Take care of your cheque book and do not keep your cheque card with it.

Post-dated cheques

A cheque dated for some time in the future will not be paid until the date stated on the cheque, and therefore a bank will refuse to accept it until that date.

Lost cheques

Occasionally, a cheque will be lost (possibly in the post). As soon as this is known the drawer should advise his bank in writing to stop payment and, after this instruction has been acknowledged, issue a duplicate cheque to the payee and notify his bank that this has been done.

Banker's draft

This is a cheque drawn up by the bank itself and, as it will be issued only if the account holder has sufficient funds, is a guarantee of payment; one case where it is used is in house purchase.

Cheque cards

These are issued by banks to approved customers and guarantee that a cheque up to £50 will be met by the bank; an increasing number of shopkeepers will now accept payment by cheque only if a cheque card is produced. Both cheque cards and credit cards (e.g. Barclaycard or Access, dealt with on page 104) are acceptable as proof of identity when a person wishes to cash a cheque at a branch other than his own.

Forged cheques
If the signature of the drawer is forged and the bank pays out its customer's money against such a cheque, it is likely to have to bear the loss itself.

Night safe
Business firms wishing to safeguard cash after banking hours may be provided with a key to the night safe outside the bank's premises, enabling them to deposit money in a specially numbered wallet which drops into the bank's vaults.

The clearing system

As a cheque is drawn on a particular branch of a bank, it can be paid only at that branch. As something like four million cheques a day are paid into 14 000 bank branches, it is obvious that a special organisation is needed to 'clear' these cheques, that is, to transfer the value from the paying branch to the collecting branch of, probably, another bank. Membership of the London *bankers' clearing house*, which does the necessary clearing of cheques and drafts, consists of the Bank of England, the six London clearing banks, together with the Co-operative Bank and the Central Trustee Savings Bank. Arrangements have now been made for the National Girobank (see Chapter 10) to join the clearing house. The clearing system is now largely computerised and is probably more advanced than any comparable system in the world. In the early part of the eighteenth century the clearing of cheques was accomplished by clerks who walked from branch to branch presenting cheques for payment and obtaining cash in exchange. From this developed the system of meeting at a central point, exchanging cheques and settling only the difference between the totals exchanged. This scheme was unofficial at first, but when the bankers themselves saw its advantages they established an official clearing house in the City of London.

For payment purposes, cheques fall into three categories:

1 Drawer and payee have accounts at the same branch of the same bank.

2   Drawer and payee have accounts at different branches of the same bank.
3   Drawer and payee have accounts at different banks.

In the first two cases, the clearing house is not involved in the settlement, as both parts of the transaction are dealt with by the same bank. It is those in group 3 (perhaps two million out of the four million cheques paid in daily) that go through the bankers' clearing house.

Basically, the general clearing procedure is as follows:

(*a*)   Each branch sorts all cheques paid in into bank order, machine-lists them, giving totals, and sends the bundles to its own clearing department in London.

(*b*)   The individual clearing departments of the clearing banks amalgamate the bundles and summarise the totals of the listings. In the past this work was done manually but, with the introduction of automation, automatic cheque-sorters and cheque-reading machines, using magnetic ink characters (referred to on page 90), have been carrying out the work at high speed.

(*c*)   Representatives take the listings to the bankers' clearing house for exchange; the actual cheques are sent direct to the head offices of the banks concerned. As a safety precaution banks micro-film all cheques paid in.

(*d*)   The reverse procedure then takes place, and bundles of cheques will be despatched by post to the branches on which they are drawn, who examine and approve for payment.

(*e*)   It will be realised that the first notification the paying bank has that one of its customers has drawn a cheque is when (*d*) occurs. It sometimes happens (either through lack of funds or because the cheque has been completed incorrectly) that the bank will not agree to pay. The cheque is then returned unpaid direct by post to the branch where it was originally paid in; that branch will then advise its customer accordingly.

At the end of each day at the clearing house, each bank prepares a *settlement sheet* showing balances due to be received from other banks against balances due to be paid to other banks. The actual settlement is effected through the account each clearing bank maintains at the Bank of England – it will be appreciated that total balances paid by the debtor banks must equal the total balances due to be received by the creditor banks.

The clearing operation normally takes several days, though sometimes longer delays occur. Special arrangements exist whereby cheques over £5000 drawn on and paid into City of London branches are cleared the same day. This materially assists the operation of the large financial institutions.

A number of cheques will be drawn on banks other than the clearing banks (e.g. the merchant banks or government departments). Again, special clearing arrangements exist to deal with these cheques.

Credit transfer (bank giro) system

For years banks have transferred money value to one another by means of credit slips. Examples are:

(a) A customer pays in money for his account at a branch other than his own.

(b) A customer has arranged for his bank to make a regular payment on his behalf to another bank for the credit of one of their customers. Examples are a fixed sum paid monthly to a building society, or an annual payment to a club or association.

(c) A business pays its employees their salaries (or its creditors the amounts due to them) by issuing one cheque payable to its own bank accompanied by credit slips giving the names, branch bank details and individual amounts due to various persons; the bank then distributes the credit slips to other banks, who credit their customers.

In 1960 these credit transfer activities were extended to include the following:

(d) A customer or a non-customer could pay in money at one branch for the credit of a customer whose account was held at a different branch or bank. Institutions like local authorities, gas boards, and so on began to incorporate a credit-transfer slip as part of the bill sent to the customer; thus the latter could either pay in cash, together with the slip, at a branch or could issue one cheque payable to his own bank covering several bills.

All the above items under (*a*) to (*d*) have since 1960 been settled through the bankers' clearing house under a credit clearing – this operates in a similar way to the general clearing already referred to. The total number of credit vouchers is rapidly increasing; currently over five million a week are dealt with. It is expected that as these increase the total of cheques will decrease. Basically, the difference between a payment by cheque and one by credit transfer (now generally called bank giro) can be summarised thus:

1   *Cheque.* The *collecting* bank initiates the transaction by crediting the payee and then asks the paying bank for the money.
2   *Giro transfer*, e.g. transaction (*b*) above. The *paying* bank initiates the transaction by deducting the money from the customer's account (debiting him) and giving it to the collecting bank, who credits its customer. This is the more logical method and, in addition, reduces costs.

Direct debiting
This is another system for settling debts without the use of cheques which has been introduced in recent years. As far as the ordinary customer is concerned, the effect of the system is the same as the standing order procedure. Technically, there are two differences. Under the standing order method, the debtor instructs his bank to pay the creditor. With direct debiting, the creditor *claims* the amount due to him direct from the debtor's bank: the debtor, of course, has to give his permission before this can be done. In effect, the payee is authorised by the debtor to write out a cheque on the latter's account himself. Secondly, unlike a standing order, the amount need not be fixed. As far as inter-business transactions are concerned, considerable use is made of the direct-debiting scheme. To enable the debtor to maintain control of his account there is an agreed interval between invoicing and debiting. For example, business A submits its monthly bill to business B on 1 January; on 15 January, unless B's bank has been instructed by him not to pay, A's bank, acting on his behalf, will claim and receive payment from B's bank. The system is operated through the inter-bank computer

bureau, and much time and labour are saved by its use. Many institutions (e.g. insurance companies) will only accept regular payments by the direct debit system. Under the standing order method the debtor has to amend his instruction to his bank each time the premium changes (a problem particularly in periods of inflation). Safeguards for the customer have been introduced in connection with direct debiting which appear to be wholly satisfactory, thus making it quite safe to sign an authority for a creditor to collect such sums as are due to him (without the amount being spelled out).

Deposit accounts

In the current account money can be paid in, withdrawn or transferred to another person without notice being given. Thus the current account is essentially used, not as a savings account, but as a readily accessible store of money value. Operating costs for the bank are high (consider the time it takes for a cashier to check physically a large sum of money) and, furthermore, the bank has no guarantee that it will have the use of the money deposited for a definite period. Thus no interest is paid normally and, as already mentioned, charges are sometimes incurred by the customer. For the benefit of the person who wishes to leave surplus money to earn interest, a deposit account is available. Seven days' notice is required of withdrawal (though generally this is waived and the withdrawal back-dated seven days instead, thus reducing interest) and no cheque books are issued. Interest varies according to the bank base rate and over the last twenty years has varied from 2% to 14% p.a. Many customers maintain both current and deposit accounts, transferring from one to the other as required. By special arrangement, large-scale depositors may negotiate a higher interest rate, often agreeing to give longer notice than seven days.

What happens to money in the bank?

The greater part of a bank's income arises from the lending of money deposited with it. Experience has shown that the banks need to keep only about 8% or 9% of their total deposits in cash – either in notes or coins at the branch or the head office, or in a current account at the Bank of England (the bankers' bank). This, of course, earns no interest. Another proportion of their money is kept in assets that can be turned into money at short notice. For example, money is lent to government departments indirectly by purchasing Treasury bills (see Chapter 8), which can themselves be traded in the money market to other financial institutions (in effect, the bill is really a legal IOU guaranteed by the government which will be paid out by them to the holder at the end of a short period, say ninety days). Interest rates on these short-term loans are low compared with those that can be earned from loans to customers. A bank will also invest in government securities – these are issued by the state to provide it with money in the medium or long term.

Borrowing from a bank

Advances are the amounts that banks lend to their customers. A higher rate of interest will be earned than on the bank's other assets, but there is a greater degree of risk involved for the banker and he will incur administrative costs in managing the advances. The interest rate will vary for different types of customers and at the time of writing (early 1983) a minimum of 12% is likely to be charged. This compares with a deposit account interest rate of about 6%. After allowing for expenses and taxation the net gain to the bank is around 1%.

The 1981/2 balance sheet of Barclays Bank shows that of a total of £16000 million owing to bank customers on current and deposit accounts, £13000 million (or 80%) had been advanced in loans and overdrafts.

The majority of bank lending is to businesses, ranging from small firms to mammoth companies, though large sums are also lent to public authorities (for example, to local councils for day-to-day expenditure pending receipt of rate income) and to private customers. From time to time in recent years, the government has by various ways restricted the total amount of bank lending or has encouraged the banks to give priority to certain types of customer, for example to exporters. Only a comparatively small proportion of total advances is made to private persons – banks nowadays encourage them to borrow from the credit card companies (Access,

Barclaycard, etc.), who will lend up to a specific credit limit to customers.

Customers borrow for a variety of reasons: the manufacturer needs 'working' finance to bridge the gap between installing plant, buying new materials, meeting the expenses of manufacturing goods and being paid for the finished product by the consumer. The farmer has similar problems. The retailer may need to carry large stocks and to give credit. The private customer may borrow to improve his house, or he may want a 'bridging loan' while the sale of one house and the purchase of another are negotiated.

Generally, banks prefer to lend for a relatively short period, but recently they have adopted more flexible lending policies and will also consider medium-term loans (fully secured) of up to seven or ten years. Bank advances are of two types:

1 *Fixed loans.* £x is lent for an agreed period (say, one year) to be repaid with interest either by regular instalments or in a lump sum at the end of the year.
2 *Overdrafts.* For the customer who wants an advance of varying amounts for limited periods (e.g. a retailer stocking up for a peak sale time or a business needing finance for a few weeks each month pending receipt of payments from trade debtors) an overdraft is more convenient than a fixed loan. The bank manager in this case agrees to allow his customer to spend more than he has in his account up to an agreed maximum. This is the cheapest form of borrowing because interest is charged only on the actual sum owing on a daily basis, though the rate per cent charged may be higher.

The bank does not want to grant speculative advances; after all, it is using its depositors' money. It therefore prefers to lend with comparative safety to honest and reliable persons or to firms who can satisfy the manager that repayment on the agreed terms is within their capabilities. A commercial bank is therefore more restrictive in its lending policy than, say, a hire-purchase finance company, and charges a lower rate of interest than the latter, which, of course, itself pays its depositors a higher interest than the bank does.

The banker may ask for some form of security. This is the right to sell some possession left with the bank – for example, stocks and shares of companies quoted on the Stock Exchange (Chapter 2), life assurance policies or deeds of property. Basically, to be acceptable the security must be one that it will be possible to store in the bank's vaults and to convert to money easily. Much lending by banks, however, is done without security, especially that to established businesses or comparatively small sums to private customers.

It is outside the scope of this book to discuss at length factors governing interest rates. Briefly, however, these can be summed up:

(*a*) The condition of the economy and the government's view on monetary matters. Until 1981 a change in Minimum Lending Rate (MLR) was taken as evidence that the authorities wished interest rates to change. The system of announcing regularly the MLR has been abandoned. Now it is the quantity of money in circulation which is given emphasis. Nevertheless, it is still a truism that high interest rates discourage borrowers and vice versa. USA interest rates exercise considerable influence on the rest of the world.

(*b*) The type of customer, the amount and period of the loan. An established company will be charged less than the author of this book; a large loan may carry a lower rate than a small loan because the servicing costs of the latter are proportionally greater; an overdraft will be charged at a lower rate per cent than a fixed sum for a set length of time because the former can be 'called in' by the bank at comparatively short notice; in other words, one pays a higher rate of interest in return for a guarantee that one will have the use of the money for a prearranged period.

Other banking services

In addition to services already mentioned in this chapter (current and deposit accounts, and advances to customers), the following facilities are available:

Safeguarding of valuables

Customers can leave important documents and valuable boxes and parcels in the bank's strongroom. Large branches may also have special safe-deposit facilities enabling the customer to have access himself to a private compartment. The police are not too happy about this as it is believed that robbery proceeds are being banked in these safe deposits.

Stock Exchange work
Banks will buy and sell all types of securities, including government bonds, on behalf of their customers. No charge is made as the stockbroker shares his normal commission with the bank.

Investment management
A specialist investment department will, for a fee, manage investment portfolios for customers.

Income Tax department
Here the bank operates as a tax accountant, dealing with taxation affairs for its customers.

Foreign exchange and travel
This service is also available to non-customers. Travellers' cheques (cashable in banks, etc. abroad) and letters of credit enabling cheques to be cashed at certain foreign banks are supplied; furthermore, a bank will arrange the obtaining of passports.

Overseas trade
The bank will deal with the complicated arrangements necessary in connection with payments for imports and exports. This service is dealt with in greater detail in Chapter 14. The bank can also arrange to settle a debt incurred overseas by an individual and send money to relatives and friends abroad.

Executor and trustee departments
Many persons ask the bank to act for them as executor after death – this means clearing up a person's estate and ensuring that his instructions as to bequests are duly carried out. If necessary, they will also act as trustees (e.g. if legal minors are involved, or if the income from property is left to someone for the duration of life only).

Registrars and new issues

All the commercial banks have a special department to carry out the complicated work involved in the issue of stocks and shares and the maintenance of shareholders' registers (see Chapter 3).

Mortgage and insurance services

In recent years the banks have extended their loan services by acting as mortgagees; that is, advancing money on a long-term basis to home purchasers against the security of the property, thus competing against building societies. However, there is now growing evidence that the banks propose to limit their activities in this field. Through their own subsidiary companies the banks now act as insurers for a variety of policies.

Advice and information

In addition to a variety of publications on economic, financial and trade conditions abroad, banks will also provide references for their own customers and make inquiries about the credit-worthiness of firms and individuals (see Chapter 7 dealing with transactions on credit). Also, since bank managers have wide financial knowledge, they are always willing to assist a customer with general advice on business matters. It is worth pointing out that the banker has a traditional duty to keep his customers' affairs a secret, though he may be compelled to supply information to the courts and police authorities.

Night safe, cash dispenser, transfers and direct debits, cheque cards

These have already been referred to earlier in this chapter.

Credit cards

These enable the card holder to obtain credit at a large number of establishments (shops, garages, transport undertakings, etc.) that have joined the scheme. The customer receives a monthly statement from the credit company and either pays in full within several weeks, thus incurring no interest charges, or makes a part payment, in which case interest is charged on the balance left owing. The seller who has given credit is paid by the credit company, which receives a commission of perhaps 2% to 4% from him. Obviously the seller hopes to increase his turnover sufficiently to offset his lower percentage profit; some people feel that the long-term effect of the credit-card system will be to increase retail prices. The two largest schemes in this country are Barclaycard (operated by the Barclay Bank group) and Access (run by a consortium of the other three major banking groups). The Barclaycard also acts as a cheque card. The increasing use of credit cards is a step nearer the 'cashless society'.

10

The Post Office; British Telecom

The postal and telecommunications businesses, formerly run by the Post Office, have, since October 1981, been operated by two completely separate corporations. Both bodies have had their monopoly powers modified so that they are now subject, increasingly, to private sector competition (see page 39).

The Post Office

Remittance services
Since the withdrawal of the inland telegraph payment facility there are only two ways of making payments through the Post Office: the postal order; and via the National Girobank, a complete banking organisation. Both these methods can also be used, subject to various conditions, for overseas payments.

Postal orders
These vouchers are sold at post offices for a variety of fixed sums from 25p to £10; a poundage charge (1982 – 26p) is made on each order to cover administrative expenses. Stamps may be added to make up the odd pence to the sum required. If the postal order is crossed (see page 91) it must be paid into a bank account for collection in the same way as a cheque, otherwise an order can be cashed by the payee at the named post office or at any post office if no address is stipulated. There is little security with an uncrossed document as, even if the payee is named, the Post Office cannot be expected to check identity. Postal orders are used by individuals

without bank accounts and in a few business areas only, for example mail order (see page 56) and football pools.

There is some safeguard for the purchaser of the postal order if it is lost in transit, because if he can produce the counterfoil (a perforated slip stating the value) he will be able to obtain – after some delay – compensation; however, unless he can establish negligence by the Post Office, he will lose his money if the order is cashed dishonestly.

The National Girobank

This is a new banking service opened by the Post Office in 1968. Basically, it provides a similar range of facilities to those available to the current account holder at a commercial bank. The Giro is mainly concerned with money deposits, withdrawals and transfers, and does not provide all the other services available to bank customers which are referred to in Chapter 9. However, additional services have now been introduced, including personal loans, budget accounts, foreign currency exchange, cheque guarantee cards and so on. A useful new service is Transcash, enabling people who do not have accounts to make cash payments to those with Girobank accounts (many organisations now incorporate Transcash forms on their bills). Increasingly this system is offered in connection with mail order (see Chapter 5).

Giros have existed in other countries for many years, largely because they lacked an efficient and comprehensive commercial banking system. The UK service, though it initially provided an excellent range of current account facilities, in many cases at a lower cost than its rivals, did not, in terms of the total number of account holders, grow as rapidly as the Post Office anticipated. To some extent this was because many persons believed that, with the change of government from Labour to Conservative in 1970, the Giro would be restricted in its activities, or even be abolished. However, with its future assured and with the introduction of the additional services referred to above, considerable expansion has taken place (1982 – one million private accounts).

The Giro service is one in which all accounts are held at a single centre (Bootle, Merseyside). So, instead of using cheques which pass from payer to payee and then have to be cleared to particular banks, payments between Giro account holders can be made by sending transfer instructions to the centre, which uses a computer system to perform the necessary clerical work at high speed and send the necessary advice to the payee by post the same day. In fact, the payee receives the actual transfer form, which can carry a message relating to the payment. This is obviously a very economical way of operating a payments system. It lends itself to computer operation; it is at its cheapest and most efficient in handling automatic payments and standing orders (these are free); and it can make the maximum use of the postal network. The only post office counter transactions that are required are when cash enters and leaves the system; this arises only when cash is deposited or withdrawn by the account holder, or when people who are not Giro account holders make payments to Giro accounts (Transcash).

The Giro has interchange arrangements with the commercial banks so that Giro account holders can issue payment orders (equivalent to a cheque), which can be cleared in the usual way, pay ordinary cheques into their Giro accounts and transfer their own funds between the two systems.

The standing order and automatic debit transfer facilities (Chapter 9) are in principle the same as those provided by the commercial banks. Customers issued with a guarantee card can withdraw up to £50 every other day at any post office; other customers must use two nominated post offices. Cheques for larger amounts need authorisation from the Giro centre. As far as transfers from one account holder to another are concerned, the Girobank is superior to the commercial banks – a simple transfer form on which a message can be included is sent by post to the Giro centre, who, after processing, pass it on to the payee. The provision of customers' statements, every day if required, is also better.

It is difficult to say to what extent the commercial banks have been adversely affected by the Giro service. It is doubtful if many businesses have closed their accounts at commercial banks. What has happened is that large numbers of firms have opened National Giro accounts while retaining their existing bank accounts, choosing the appropriate system for any particular type of transaction. Special services for business customers have been introduced, including collection of rents for housing authorities and salary payment facilities. A regional structure for National Giro banking, with offices in many cities, has been set up.

Communications services of the Post Office

The Post Office, in addition to providing money transmission services and a variety of savings and investment facilities, is the main agent for communications channels for the written word, and an important transporter of parcels. As such, it is a very vital part of the chain of commerce. It is still one of the largest employers of labour in the country, even after the hiving off of British Telecom, and the total capital invested in the industry is phenomenal.

The Post Office is a main link in the myriad communications made daily by both business and the private citizen; for example, 10 000 million letters and parcels are handled annually. The Post Office has a monopoly on the conveyance of letters but, as already mentioned, the Secretary of State for Industry has powers to allow private competition in certain circumstances.

The Post Office Guide, published annually, sets out in detail all the services that are available; a brief outline is given below of the major ones, many of them being available on a worldwide basis. Any prices indicated below are correct as at February 1983.

Postal services

Letters

For some years there has been a two-tier service, second-class mail being cheaper, on average twenty-four hours slower and only available up to a certain maximum weight. At present, charges depend on weight, but in the future, when the sorting process is wholly mechanised, size will also be taken into account since items that do not conform to certain limits of measurement, called Post Office preferred sizes, will require hand-sorting.

Registration and recorded delivery

These are two 'insurance' services which provide compensation if a letter or packet is lost in transit. The former carries compensation of up to £1500, and items like money and jewellery are permissible. Recorded delivery is very much cheaper than registration and is ideal for legal documents, certificates, and so on, where it is important for both parties to have a post office receipt, even though the documents have little monetary value. Recorded delivery pays compensation up to £18 only, and money and jewellery are excluded.

Limited compensation may also be available for ordinary letters lost or damaged provided a certificate of posting is obtained. 'Consequential loss' insurance (a loss over and above the article lost, damaged or delayed when sent by registered post) has now been introduced. An example would be a passport, which if lost in the post could mean a delayed business trip and the loss of a contract.

Business reply service and freepost

Both these services enable a person or firm to receive cards or letters from clients without prepayment of postage by the latter. In each case, a licence, for which a fee is charged annually, is necessary and a very small fee in addition to normal postage is paid by the addressee. The points of difference between the two are:

(*a*)   Business reply service is available in first- and second-class services, but freepost is second-class only.

(*b*)   The envelope, card or label used in the business reply service must be of a special design and colour.

In both cases, the licensee has to make an advance payment covering the estimated charges in the following month and renew his credit when this sum is exhausted.

Express and other special services

For payment of an extra fee, letters and small packets can be delivered by special messenger over part or all of their journey. Railway and air letters can also be sent; in each case, the letter has to be handed in at the station or airport.

Parcel post

The Post Office carries vast quantities of parcels and this service is of great importance to many businesses, for example, mail order. There are both weight (10 kg) and size limits, and a lower area rate charge is made for parcels posted and delivered within a certain group of counties (e.g. Dorset and Hampshire). An insurance scheme now operates to cover losses or damage in transit. Cash-on-delivery facilities are also available, the Post Office collecting up to

£300 from the addressee in return for a small fee paid by the sender. A postage forward parcel service, similar in principle to the business reply service for letters, is also operated.

Datapost

Datapost, available only on a contract basis with individual charges negotiated, provides a reliable, fast, overnight service (including collection and delivery at agreed times) of special classes of goods such as urgent computer data, salary and wage records, medicines and vital hospital equipment. There is also a service to the USA offering next-day delivery to certain towns.

Miscellaneous

A wide range of other facilities are afforded the business firm. Selectapost enables mail to be pre-sorted by the Post Office for the addressee into appropriate departments if these are suitably indicated; private boxes can be rented at the normal delivery office so that collection can be made as an alternative to delivery by postmen; free collection from firms of letters and parcels can be arranged subject to certain minimum quantities; franking machines can be rented from approved private firms, or postage can be prepaid in money for bulk postings.

The economics of the postal services

As these operations are still labour intensive, the cost of the provision of facilities is high and for some years serious financial losses have been incurred, aggravated by the fact that successive governments have expected the nationalised industries to pay their way, while restricting their right to charge an economic price for their services.

At present, most sorting has to be done by hand, but gradually the Post Office intends to mechanise the whole operation using the post-code service. Eventually this will save labour, but in the meantime high capital sums will be needed for the installation of the necessary computerised equipment; thus postal charges are unlikely to be reduced.

British Telecommunications (BT)

Britain has the world's fourth largest telecommunications with 28 million telephones, 90000 telex connections and over 80000 data transmission terminals (the USA is the only country with a greater number). British Telecom, established under the 1981 Act already referred to, operates these telecommunications and data processing services with a staff of a quarter of a million people, 50000 vehicles and total assets of £16000 million. In line with its 'privatisation' policy, the 1979 Conservative government began to allow private enterprise to supply equipment (with the exception of the customers' first telephones) as well as the provision of various services via the public network, such as computer bureaus.

The transmission by physical means of the written word has been dealt with, and the transmission of freight is discussed in considerable detail in Chapter 12. Now the services providing *instant* communication of the spoken and written word must be considered. These facilities are of particular importance in helping to ensure the smooth running of business life, while at the same time being a considerable convenience to us all in our private lives. It is the provision of and the improvements to the telecommunications services that have provided, in many circumstances, a better method of information communication than has been possible by post.

Telephones

Virtually all subscribers now have access to subscriber trunk dialling (STD) channels, enabling them to dial direct to numbers both in this country and, increasingly, abroad. Charges are costed on a time and distance basis, with lower rates at certain times of the day. The introduction of the system has meant that long-distance calls of short duration can be made cheaply. For example, an office in Edinburgh calling Birmingham would pay 20p for a one-minute call in the afternoon.

Most businesses will have their own internal switchboards, and if private automatic branch exchange (PABE) equipment is used, external calls from extensions do not require the help of the operator. A few very large organisations, such as the Greater London Council, have direct dialling in, enabling outside callers to dial the required extension direct – an enormous labour-saving facility.

Various sophisticated types of equipment are now available which speed up call connection. Callmakers obviate the need for manual dialling and re-dialling by storing either small or large numbers of telephone numbers on card or tape.

A variety of telephone services are offered by British Telecom, including:

(a) *Transferred charge calls*. Cost charged to the called subscriber with his permission.

(b) *Telephone credit cards*. A card holder can have calls from any telephone charged to his regular telephone account.

(c) *Personal calls*. In return for payment of a fee, the timing of a call does not start till the required person is available. Since the introduction of STD this service has been less used.

(d) *Telephone answering service*. The equipment will automatically record calls while a telephone is unmanned.

(e) *Radiophone*. This is a public mobile radio telephone scheme for use in vehicles in certain areas only, and enables calls to be both received and made. Radio paging is now available throughout the UK.

(f) *Private telephone lines*. Direct lines can be installed to allow communication between two or more points without using the public system. These circuits can also be used for the transmission of data, alarm signals, pictures and music.

(g) *Telephone directories*. In addition to alphabetical directories, the Post Office issues classified business (Yellow Pages) and other commercial classified directories. Mention was made in Chapter 7 of their use in connection with obtaining details of potential suppliers of goods.

(h) *Freefone*. This service enables clients, agents and employers to call the Freefone subscriber via the operator: the subscriber is billed for the call in the usual way.

Telegrams and telemessages
The inland telegram service ended in 1982 after 112 years. From a peak of 63 million telegrams in 1945 numbers dwindled to 2 million in 1981, caused by the increasing use of the telephone. The telemes-

sage, which has replaced the overnight telegram service, now provides an adequate alternative. International telegrams continue to be available via telephone or telex.

Telex
This system enables a copy of a message to be produced on teleprinters at both the sending and the receiving installations. The United Kingdom service is wholly automatic, subscribers dialling direct anywhere in the country. About 98% of all overseas calls can also be directly dialled. In addition to the advantage of having a written rather than an oral message, information can be received even though the teleprinter is unattended. Although the present minimum rental is comparatively expensive, the charge for calls, if a skilled typist is used, is rather less than that of the equivalent telephone conversation. Private teleprinter links are also available, and high-speed transmission of prepunched tape is possible. There are over 90 000 subscribers in the UK and over one million in other parts of the world.

Datel
Data prepared for computer use on prepunched tape may be transmitted over the telex or telephone type circuits. Thus a branch office can send data at high speed to its computer centre. An alternative service to Datel called PSS is also available. It is a new public network, like the telephone network, but it is provided exclusively for carrying data. It will also allow interconnection between terminals working at different speeds and also to other parts of the world.

Prestel
Prestel links the television set and the telephone and enables the subscriber to 'call-up' on his set a very wide range of business, social and other information. There are thousands of 'pages' of data available.

Future development
Further progress in the use of satellites will materially improve oral, visual and written communication with distant countries. The visual

telephone system is likely to be introduced commercially within a few years. The use of ordinary telephone circuits to receive television or to read electricity and gas meters (without preventing simultaneous normal telephone conversations) is likely. Facsimile transmission of actual documents over telephone lines, already in use (Bureaufax), will be further developed.

With the rapid strides being made in the fields of both transport and telecommunications, those readers who live to see the twenty-first century will indeed witness what a few decades ago would have been described as miracles.

11

Accounting Principles

The capital of a business

In the accounting sense, *capital* means the 'net worth' of a business, the value of its property and possessions (called *assets*) less the amounts owing to its creditors (called *liabilities*). This is called the *accounting equation:*

$$\text{Capital} = \text{assets } less \text{ liabilities}$$

Every transaction must have an equal and opposite effect on the equation. The statement setting out the net worth is described as a *balance sheet* and, although those wishing to study elementary accounting are recommended to read a book such as *Book-keeping* in the Teach Yourself series, nevertheless all persons studying a commerce text ought to understand a few basic principles. Remember that the form in which accounts may be set out may vary tremendously; it is their meaning that is important.

Effect of transactions on a balance sheet

The balance sheet is really a picture of the business at any moment – imagine a movie camera making a running record of what is happening as various transactions take place. For example, if a delivery van is purchased and paid for by cheque, then the business *acquires* a van (asset plus) and *cash at bank* is reduced (asset minus). In practice, separate accounts will be kept to record the different types of transaction and a balance sheet drawn up at the end of the accounting period to show the cumulative effect of all the transactions in that period (probably a year). However, the 'movements' on the balance sheet can be illustrated as each transaction is effected and thus show the state of the firm at that moment in time.

Day 1
R.W. opens business with £15000 in Bank.

BALANCE SHEET DAY 1

Owner's capital	£15000	Cash at bank	£15000

Remember the equation

$$C = A - L$$
$$£15000 = £15000 - Nil$$

Day 2
(*a*) Equipment bought for £1600 and paid for by cheque.
(*b*) Goods for resale (called stock) bought on credit for £700 from AKC Ltd.

BALANCE SHEET DAY 2

		Assets	
Owner's capital	£15000	Equipment	£ 1600
		Bank £15000 − £1600	£13400
		Stock	£ 700
			£15700
		Less liabilities	
		Creditor AKC Ltd	£ 700
	£15000	Net worth	£15000

Owner's capital (though not his cash) remains the same: (*a*) merely exchanges one asset for another; (*b*) an asset is acquired with an equal and opposite liability.

Day 3
R.W. pays various expenses totalling £200.

BALANCE SHEET DAY 3

		Assets	
Capital	£15 000	Equipment	£ 1 600
Less expenses	£ 200	Bank £13 400 − £200	£13 200
		Stock	£ 700
	————		————
			£15 500
		Less liabilities	
		Creditor AKC Ltd	£ 700
	————		————
	£14 800		£14 800

Here his capital reduces because he pays out cash and, although he obtains a service (e.g. wages, advertising, rates, etc), he acquires no tangible possession in exchange.

Day 4
(a)   He sells his stock for £1020 to ABC & Co on credit (they become a debtor).
(b)   He pays AKC Ltd £500 on account.

BALANCE SHEET DAY 4

			Assets	
Capital		£15 000	Equipment	£ 1 600
Add profit	£320		Bank £13 200 − £500	£12 700
Less expenses	£200	£ 120	Stock	Nil
			Debtor ABC & Co	£ 1 020
		————		————
				£15 320
			Less creditor	
			AKC Ltd £700 − £500	£ 200
		————		————
		£15 120		£15 120

(a) Illustrates the first increase in capital. The debtor is included as an asset because £1020 is legally due to R.W. The asset *stock* reduces by £700 and the asset *debtor* is substituted at £1020 – so total assets increase by £320.

(*b*) Paying AKC Ltd reduces cash at bank but reduces a liability by the same amount, so there is no difference in capital.

From the above illustrations it will therefore be seen that:

1 Capital decreases when expenses are paid and increases when goods are sold at a profit. The total of all the profit items less the expense (or loss) items gives us total net profit for the period. In the above case, it is £120 and therefore net worth has increased by this sum; note that the profit is not in cash, it is tied up in the assets. Thus:

Day 1	Net assets	£15 000
Day 4	Net assets	£15 120
Increase in net assets		
(or net worth)		£120 = Net profit for the 4 days

2 When we buy or sell goods we record the transaction, even though we have not paid, or have not been paid, for the goods. So creditors (sums we will have to pay out in the future) are counted as *liabilities* as soon as they are incurred and debtors (sums we are due to receive in the future) are counted as assets in the same way.

3 Expenses mean overhead or running costs of the business (examples given above). Items such as equipment, delivery vans or the buildings themselves which the business buys, not with the intention of selling but to use (probably for many years) in the operation of the business, are called *fixed assets* and are not deducted from the profit in one lump sum as the expenses are. Instead, their initial cost is spread over their life in the accounts; thus a machine costing £10 000 lasting ten years will be spread over ten years' accounts, a certain percentage being regarded as an expense each year. This is called *depreciation* (see page 126).

Interpretation of a simple balance sheet

BALANCE SHEET OF ANITA'S HAIRDRESSING SALON AT
31 MARCH 1983

	£		£	£
Capital 1.4.82	65 000	*Fixed assets*		
Add		Freehold premises	63 000	
Net profit for year	10 000	Shop fittings	3 000	
	75 000			66 000
Less				
Drawings in year	5 100	*Current assets*		
		Stock for sale	800	
		Debtors	200	
		Bank deposit account	3 000	
		Bank current account	300	
			4 300	
		Less		
		Current liabilities		
		Creditors	400	
				3 900
	£69 900			£69 900

Notes

(*a*) *Drawings* means money the owner has taken out of the business for her personal use in the year. Anita has wisely left £4900 in the business, it has been ploughed back and the capital therefore increases by this sum.

(*b*) Current assets and current liabilities – items that are continually changing as the business operates. The excess of the former over the latter is called *working* or *circulating capital*. It is important for the well-being of the business that this is as high as possible; it will be realised that the fixed assets are 'values' that cannot be utilised, since they must be left untouched to enable the business to run.

(*c*) Deposit and current accounts – dealt with in Chapter 9. The deposit account will earn interest for the owner.

(*d*) Net profit as a percentage of owner's capital – this is one useful guideline to the success of the business:

$$\frac{10\,000}{65\,000} \times 100 = \text{(approximately) } 15\%$$

Bear in mind that the sole trader here is the risk taker – she is obviously entitled to a higher yield than she could earn if she merely invested her capital in a safe security (which might pay up to 8%). Also, if she is herself working in the business, she obviously wishes to earn a salary.

(*e*)   Stock is normally valued at its cost price (see later) as profit must not be anticipated – it is only when a sale is made that the profit element is taken into the accounts.

Loan capital

This is also referred to in Chapter 2 in connection with limited liability companies. Many sole traders (and partnerships) also borrow money for a fixed period of years to enable them to expand their businesses. Naturally, the borrower hopes that his return or yield expressed as a percentage will be somewhat greater than the interest rate he will have to pay the lender – though, of course, it may be several years before increased profits materialise.

Assuming our hairdressing business on 1 April 1983 borrowed £25 000 from the bank, possibly secured against the freehold premises by mortgage, a balance sheet made out immediately the loan was received would be as follows (summarised):

BALANCE SHEET AT 1 APRIL 1983

	£		£
Capital 31.3.83	69 900	Fixed assets	66 000
Mortgage loan	25 000	Current assets	
(repayable in 1998)		*Less* current liabilities	
		(i.e. working capital)	28 900
	£94 900		£94 900

The business has greater total assets than hitherto, but the owner's capital has not increased. We call the mortgage loan fixed capital because it is available for a good many years before due for repayment. At the present time (1983), around 12% interest would be charged on this type of mortgage on commercial premises, which means that unless the owner can use the money borrowed to add more than £3000 annually to her profits she is not making good economic use of the money.

Turnover: profits and losses

It has already been seen that inevitably there must be a time-lag between the purchase of the materials, goods and services needed to produce goods ready for sale and the actual receipt of proceeds from the sale. If the cost of purchases of goods only is considered, it will be seen that if a firm spends £5000 on buying stock on 1 January, pays for it on 31 January and sells the goods on 31 March, receiving settlement on 30 April, then there has been a three-month gap (31 January to 30 April) between expenditure and income; arithmetically, therefore, £5000 has been tied up without interest for this period – a loss of £100 (calculated at 8% p.a.). This example, oversimplified though it is, will serve to show that the businessman will try to achieve the highest possible *rate of turnover* he can – that is, the measurement of the speed at which goods are sold. For example, if a fishmonger receives a supply of fish every morning and always sells it the same day, then his stock is turned over once a day and we say that his rate of turnover (or *stockturn*) is 1 per day. If I own a small car sales business and always keep 3 cars in stock, then if I sell 36 cars in a year my stock has turned over 12 times in the year – because the 3 cars have been replaced on 12 occasions.

Calculation of rate of turnover

The above two examples, while illustrating the principle, will hardly occur in practice, for I will be selling cars individually and often there will only be one or two in stock. Similarly, the fishmonger will almost certainly have stock unsold which may be kept until the following day. In practice, therefore, the calculation is made using the value of the goods and not the actual numbers of articles.

The value of the stock in hand is taken at regular intervals depending on the type of business, and the average figure is divided into the value of the sales at *cost price* (selling price cannot be used because of the element of profit).

Example
Stock unsold: 1 January £2100; 1 April £3200; 1 July £1900; 1 October £2400; therefore average stock is £2400.

Sales during year	£10 800
Less profit (assume 33½% on SP)	£ 3 600
	£ 7 200

Rate of turnover $= \dfrac{7200}{2400} = 3$ (i.e. goods are in stock on average for 4 months as they are turned over 3 times in a year).

If detailed stock records are kept, the rate of turnover can be calculated for different departments of a business. To get real value from the figures it is necessary to compare rates of turnover over a period of several years. In trades dealing with perishables the rate is, of course, a very high one; and it is high on all food items and in many convenience goods. Naturally, where durables are concerned, for example furniture, radios and tools, the rate tends to be generally low and therefore the *margin* added to cost price will be a comparatively high one since capital is tied up for a long time.

Calculation of profit

Gross profit
If the price obtained for the goods is greater than the cost of the goods, then there is a gross profit (i.e. the profit before deducting the overhead and running expenses of the business); if the goods purchased have to be processed in any way – for instance, repacked into smaller lots – then these costs must be included. In a business selling a service, for example car repairing, then it is the cost of the materials used, plus the labour costs involved in using the materials, that is taken into account. The following example, for the sake of simplicity, takes into account only the actual cost of the goods:

TRADING ACCOUNT FOR MARCH

		£
Purchases in March – 800 items at £1		= 800
Less unsold stock at 31 March – 350 at £1		= 350
		450
Cost of goods sold		
Sales – 300 at £1.25	£375	
150 at £1.20	£180	
		555
	Gross profit	£105

Proof: 300 sold at £0.25 profit on each	£75	
150 sold at £0.20 profit on each	£30	£105

In effect, it is the profit on the goods *actually* sold that is counted; the unsold stock is transferred forward to the next accounting period at cost price (occasionally below cost price – for example, an out-of-date model which will have to be sold at a loss).

Referring to the example above, the April account would therefore commence with the £350 unsold stock from March, thus:

TRADING ACCOUNT FOR APRIL

	£
Unsold stock (from March)	350
Purchases in April (say)	1040
Goods available for sale in April	1390
Less unsold stock 30 April	490(*a*)
Cost of goods sold	900(*b*)
Sales (say)	1200
Gross profit £	300

Notes
(*a*)   This figure would be arrived at by doing a physical check.
(*b*)   If the total value of goods available for sale was £1390 and at the end of the month £490 worth remained, the remainder must have been disposed of.

Expenses or costs

The gross profit shown above has not taken account of the expenses or costs of doing business. These expenses can be subdivided into two classes:

1 *Fixed*. Basically, these are the expense items that remain constant even if the level of production varies. Examples are rent, rates, telephone *rental*, insurance of buildings, certain salaries (e.g. the manager's).
2 *Variable*. Those overheads that change as the level of production changes, e.g. power costs, salaries and wages of staff connected with production, delivery charges, telephone charges (but not the rental), and so on.

Some of these variable expenses will increase or decrease roughly in the same percentage that output rises or falls. In other cases, the percentage may differ. For example, overtime rates of pay are likely to be higher, and therefore it will be more expensive to produce each unit of the goods; similarly, petrol and maintenance costs of running delivery vehicles will not exactly double merely because sales double. Every business tries to increase its production by a greater percentage than that suffered by its expenses. There may well come a point when, because of spiralling costs, it is not worth trying to increase production. Consider the following example:

	No. of items produced	Production cost per item £	Average selling price £	Overhead expenses per item £	Profit per item £	Total profit £
Jan	1000	10.00	14	2.20	1.80	1800
Feb	1200	9.90	14	2.10	2.00	2400
March	1600	12.00	14	2.30	(Loss) 0.30	(Loss) 480

Profit is maximised at the February production figure; to increase output above 1200 per month will probably involve considerably higher wage rates.

Net profit

After arriving at his gross profit the businessman will need to calculate his net (or real) profit by deducting his expenses. These are those items where the value of the service received is 'used up' in the accounting period in question, examples being salaries, printing, stationery and advertising, rent, rates, telephone, heating and lighting, repairs. In all cases, the amount due for the period must be taken into account, not the amount actually paid. So if we have paid £127 for building repairs but owe another £23 at the end of the period, then the correct charge to be included is £150. Conversely, if we have arranged a two-year contract for advertising for £1000, then only £500 must be included in each year. Purchases and sales are all included, whether paid for or not – the balance sheet (see page 120) will show whether there are any debtors or creditors.

An example showing the calculation of net profit might be as follows:

PROFIT AND LOSS ACCOUNT
FOR YEAR ENDED 31 MARCH, 1983

	£	£
Gross profit		20 900
Expenditure		
Rent, rates, heating and lighting	4 160	
Salaries	3 930	
Printing, stationery and advertising	1 384	
Telephone	617	
Miscellaneous office expenses	1 213	
Vehicle operating costs	1 526	
Depreciation of vehicles and equipment	750(*a*)	
Bad debts	105(*b*)	
		13 685
Net profit (*c*)		£ 7 215

Notes

(*a*) Depreciation was briefly referred to on page 120. As fixed assets will last some years, their cost is spread over the accounts for the whole period. This inevitably involves some adjustment when the item concerned is disposed of, because there cannot but help be some element of guesswork in the calculation.

Example. A motor car for a sales representative is purchased for £5000. Each year a 20% depreciation charge calculated on cost is entered on the books. As often happens, the vehicle is sold secondhand after a few years (in part exchange), and in this case £1600 is received for it early in the fourth year of ownership.

	Depreciation expense charged £	£	Book value £
End of year 1	1000	(⅕ of 5000)	4000
End of year 2	1000		3000
End of year 3	1000		2000
Adjustment year 4	400		Nil (2000 − 1600 − 400)
	£3400		

The actual capital cost of £3400 (i.e. £5000–£1600) has been spread over four years' accounts. The system of charging depreciation shown in this example is called the fixed instalment method and is the one commonly in use for assets like vehicles and equipment.

(*b*)   Bad debts. It was stated above that the value of all sales is included in the calculation of profit whether paid for or otherwise. Occasionally, despite a rigid credit-control system (see page 69), a debtor is unable to meet his commitments and may be forced to close down. The sum not received must be shown as an expense, as it was previously shown as income (in the total sales figure).

(*c*)   Taxation has been ignored here, but is of course an important factor in the accounts of a business.

12

Transport

The background

Transport is a live subject, often hitting the headlines, and the student is kept fully occupied keeping pace with the numerous White papers on freight and passenger transport. New ideas and methods are being discussed and sometimes put into operation; one constantly hears words like containerisation, unit load, rapid transport systems, freight-liner which were almost unknown a mere decade ago.

Transport improves the standard of living of the community by widening the market; it bridges the gap between raw materials and factory, and between factory and market. Efficient transport means greater division of labour; it leads to cheaper and speedier methods of production – essential to a sophisticated modern society. It is a subject to which governments are closely sensitive, for it is close to the political and economic life of the nation. First-class transport also reflects the status and prestige of a country, and enables citizens to travel easily, thereby assisting to create a more intelligent populace.

But it was not always so. In the Middle Ages communications were poor – only the Church paid any attention to the maintenance of the old Roman roads. It was the Highways Act of 1555 that gave the responsibility for road repairs to the parishes. But generally speaking, maintenance of roads was ineffective until 1835, when the principle of highways rates was introduced.

Owing to the poor state of the roads, coastal shipping and inland waterways flourished, and the latter part of the eighteenth century was the golden age of canal construction. Many of these canals became effective monopolies of inland bulk transportation, since limited water prevented duplication and the deplorable state of the roads prevented any effective competition. In the absence of any statutory control large profits were made, and this explains the suspicion with which the railways were met when their development began.

The earliest railways were private carriageways for the purpose of carrying coal from the mines to the nearest canal. The rapid growth of the railways into a predominant form of transport was due to the technical efficiency of steam locomotion, and they soon began to operate in competition with the canals. The early development had no overall plan. Lines were constructed to deal with local traffic without provision for through-traffic (there were three different gauges in use). Furthermore, the formation of a railway company necessitated a private Act of Parliament, and this was often made expensive by local opposition. In 1844 a Select Committee (under the chairmanship of Gladstone) resulted in the Railway Regulation Act, which required all companies to provide at least one train a day with third-class accommodation, travelling at not less than twelve miles an hour, the fare not to exceed one penny a mile – the famous Parliamentary train! However, the early railway legislation failed to take any positive steps to achieve coordination between railway interest and did little more than protect the narrow interests of the trader consigning goods, and the life and limb of passengers.

The provision of reasonable facilities for through-traffic was made mandatory by the Railway and Canal Traffic Act of 1854, which also included the famous 'undue preference clause' which required that, where a concession was given to one trader, the same facility must be given to any other trader requiring a similar service. This robbed the railways of a good deal of commercial freedom; it replaced economic criteria as a basis for railway charges and remained so for a hundred years.

Decline of canals

With the coming of the railways, the use of canals declined, largely owing to the failure of management to achieve the technical improvements and standardisation necessary to match the technical efficiency of the railways, and they have never recovered their position. Today, inland waterways (unlike those in Germany and Holland) are not important freight carriers, and no major change is likely in the near future.

However, the government is now prepared to make grants to help companies switch heavy traffic from the road to the waterways. Limited improvement expenditure is being incurred on canals at the moment, with a view to increasing both commercial and leisure trade. The government is also considering a fifty year scheme to develop nearly 2000 miles of canal, but no firm decision is likely in the immediate future. It is a fact that the low cost of waterway transport makes economic sense and beats the cost of road or rail transport for many goods. Slower it may be, but with many consignments a regular delivery is more important than speed.

Revival of road competition
After 1850 there was a slow revival of road transport, but horse-drawn vehicles were obviously inferior to the railways. Steam-driven coaches might have proved to be the answer if they had not caused great damage to the roads. Also, the maximum speed was four miles per hour, each vehicle had to be preceded by a man carrying a red flag, and from 1878 a licence fee of £10 had to be paid to each council within whose area the vehicle was to operate.

The advent of the internal combustion engine led to much discontent with these restrictions and they were finally abolished in 1905. This resulted in rapid replacement of horses by motor vehicles, and by 1911 the London General Omnibus Company had completely replaced its 18000 horses by motor buses.

Railways during the First World War
During the First World War the railways' resources were seriously depleted; locomotives and rolling stock were sent in large quantities to the European battlefields. From the operational point of view, the railways achieved all that was required of them and the unified operational control yielded considerable technical benefits. The financial return was far less satisfactory and at the end of the war was worse than ever.

Railways between 1919 and 1939
The first job of the Ministry of Transport (formed in 1919) was the restoration of the railway finances. Compensation was paid for any

deterioration of assets during the war period and 100% increase in the rates charged was authorised, but the coal strike of 1921 caused £60 million loss to the railways in that year alone. In these exceptionally difficult circumstances, the railways were returned to private control by the 1921 Act, which invested the railway assets in four regional companies and introduced a new rates structure. These new standard charges were not to be altered without the consent of the railways rates tribunal, except in the case of reduction of up to 40% of the standard rates, these rates to be known as 'exceptional' rates. The depressed inter-war years were difficult ones for the railways, and by 1935 the number of exceptional rates accounted for 80% of the tonnage carried. The railways never secured the 'standard' revenue (defined as the net revenue in 1913 plus additions for extra capital acquired since that date). Commercial freedom was severely restricted and the tonnage of general merchandise carried by the railways had, by 1938, declined by one third.

Control of road transport
The Ministry of Transport was responsible for organising a national roads system. The Roads Act 1920 set up a Road Fund into which all licence fees and petrol duties were to be paid for the purpose of maintaining roads.

The rapid increase of road traffic in the 1920s gave rise to concern, both because of the danger to public safety from the relatively heavy uncontrolled traffic and because of the suspicion that this expansion was at the expense of the railways, whose commercial freedom was subject to various controls. The Road Traffic Act 1930 introduced compulsory third party insurance (see Chapter 13), and the Road and Rail Act 1933 introduced a road-haulage system which lasted until the 1968 Transport Act.

The 1933 Act did impose some restrictions on the entry of new firms into road haulage, but this made it a relatively comfortable field for existing operators because the railways' decline still continued, accentuated by the depression of heavy industries – the most profitable of companies, the Southern, only paid a dividend of ½% in 1938.

London Passenger Transport Board

In 1933 the London Passenger Transport Board was established with a local monopoly (excluding taxis and main-line railways). This experiment in co-ordination was generally regarded as a success, but eventually there were alarming deficits (partly because of government control of fares and the cost of road congestion), and in 1971 the Minister of Transport, after writing off the outstanding capital debt, invested financial control in the Greater London Council. Deficit problems remain, however.

Transport during the Second World War

Government control and operation of the railways was similar to that during the 1914–18 War, and a railway executive committee composed of railway managers was responsible for operation and a fixed annual net revenue was paid.

Control of road transport was adopted to restrict it to short distances in order to conserve petrol supplies; in fact, implementation of this policy proved difficult.

The bulk of the war transport burden fell on the railways, which proved equal to the task; but war-time conditions meant a decrease in the rolling stock and engines in good repair, and in 1947 the British Transport Commission took over a railway system that was ageing and badly run-down.

The railways since 1945

The 1947 Transport Act set up the British Transport Commission (BTC) with a general duty 'to provide an efficient, adequate, economical and properly integrated system of public inland transport and road facilities'. The assets of the four railway companies were transferred to the British Transport Commission at the prevailing Stock Exchange value, which was most generous in the circumstances, and thus the BTC was committed to very heavy annual interest repayments. No arrangements were made to deal with the back-log of replacement of assets that had run down in the war years; it was assumed that for a nationalised body the necessary funds would be forthcoming! But, in fact, the Labour Government, facing economic difficulties, was unable to do so to the extent required and by 1960 railway investment (in real terms) had not caught up with the disinvestment of the war and post-war years.

The 1947 Act required the BTC to conduct its affairs so that revenue taking one year with another would be sufficient to meet costs. The BTC had to submit its charges structure to the Transport Tribunal, which had complete power over fares and charges until 1953. There was no clear indication as to what was meant by 'taking one year with another', so the tribunal could always refer to the 'long term' when making decisions immediately injurious to railway finances.

There was the problem of frequent delays, and of modifications of both freight and passenger charges schemes. Also, it was not made clear under the 1947 Act what the railway executive's responsibility was regarding social service obligations, such as keeping open lines that could not possibly pay economically but needed to remain open for the benefit of the public (i.e. in rural areas). Many railway men have always regarded this as a self-imposed obligation.

For the reasons outlined above, the railways encountered many difficulties during the period following nationalisation, and although there were operating surpluses from 1948 to 1955 these were more than offset by the losses which have continued ever since.

As a result of a change of government in 1951, there was a new policy for transport, which included some decentralisation of railway administration and a partial return to private enterprise of long-distance haulage. The Transport Act of 1943 and the Transport (Disposal of Road Haulage Property) Act 1956 put these plans into effect.

The Transport Act 1962 reorganised nationalised transport. The British Transport Commission was dissolved, and its duties and responsibilities were divided between four boards: British Railways Board, British Transport Docks Board, London Transport Board and the Transport Holding Company. The last-named was to co-ordinate the activities of certain bus companies, road hauliers, travel agencies and road freight shipping services. The Act gave considerable commercial freedom to the Railways Board, and a transport consultative committee was to report to the minister on hardship caused by the withdrawal of passenger services. Each board would be responsible for its own financial affairs; accumulated losses of nearly £500 million were written off; and the Minister of Transport was authorised to meet operating losses of £450 million over the following five years.

Improvements in railways

From the late 1950s there was a complete change from steam to diesel and electric traction; although capital cost is greater, the diesel engine is more efficient. There have also been large-scale track and signalling improvements.

By the early 1960s it had become obvious that the decrease of both goods and passenger traffic had not been halted. In 1963 the British Railways Board published its controversial report *The Reshaping of British Railways* (the Beeching Report), some of the main recommendations being:

1   Closure of many branch lines and a third of all stations.
2   Withdrawal of many stopping services.
3   Shedding of uneconomic goods traffic and closure of many freight depots.
4   Introduction of liner trains.

Steady progress was made with the rationalisation of goods traffic by the liner train concept and 'company' trains, but the withdrawal of uneconomic passenger services and the closure of stations was slowed down by considerable opposition and in the end some of the closure plans were abandoned.

Decline in rail freight

The railways' share of the freight market has dropped considerably since the Second World War. In 1952 British Railways carried in ton-mileage terms (1 ton carried 1 mile is 1 ton-mile) just over 40% of all freight within the United Kingdom. By 1970 this had declined to about 20%. In 1975, 65% of freight travelled by road, 17% by rail, 15% by coastal shipping and 3% by pipeline and inland waterway. The 1981 figures show that just under 10% of goods (by volume) were carried by rail, 82% by road, the remainder by coastal shipping, pipeline and inland waterway.

The decline in rail traffic is due mainly to two reasons:

1   A large drop in production of rail-orientated industries such as coal and steel.

2 Increasing competition from road haulage.

Freightliners and Speedlink

Attraction of more merchandise through freightliner expansion was the main hope of counteracting lost coal tonnage. These are trains made up of standardised rail cars designed to carry standard-size containers operating on a high-speed basis with no marshalling. The first freightliner service was introduced between London and Glasgow in November 1965, and in the first full year of operation 27000 containers were carried. The rate of growth is illustrated by the fact that in 1971 a million containers were carried and in the early 1970s the growth continued.

Recently a network of scheduled Speedlink high-speed services has been introduced which, by allowing for more intensive use of rolling stock, has reduced costs. Government grants have been made available towards the costs of privately-owned rail freight facilities in cases where there are considerable environmental benefits to be gained by moving heavy goods vehicle traffic from the roads. However, the proportion of freight carried by rail has continued to decline.

Concept of unit load – containers

The concept of *unit load*, particularly containerisation, is based on the principle that one large unit is speedier and easier to handle than numerous smaller items. This does not seem revolutionary, but what is new is the concept of a universally standardised container which can be carried with a minimum of trouble by rail, road and sea, and can be easily transferred from one kind of transport to another. A container is lifted off the freightliner or lorry by special equipment and transferred to the ship by straddle carrier and gantry crane. Thus containerised cargo handled by automated methods can be loaded and unloaded at the port with great speed, enabling each ship to make more voyages. Large, modern, cellular ships with space fully utilised by containers can carry much more cargo than conventional ships and the number of vessels needed on each route is greatly reduced.

Containerisation requires an investment of millions of pounds, not only in specially constructed, purpose-built vessels and containers themselves but also in port facilities, specialised cranes and handling equipment, and computers to keep track of units and to allocate space within the vessels.

Developments in shipping

In shipping there has been a trend to larger carrying units; a number of giant tankers are in service and many more are under construction. The larger the ship, the lower the unit cost of cargo carried – for operating costs do not increase in proportion to size of ship.

The necessity for larger vessels, plus the container revolution, has meant a geographical reorientation of trade routes. The closing of the Suez Canal by Egypt for some years after the 1967 Israel–Egypt War speeded up the process; although the canal was re-opened, it is far too narrow for the largest modern ships. Concentration of cargo into fewer but larger units, taken with the high cost of converting a port to the utilisation of automatic techniques, means that fewer ports will be needed. The necessity for combining trade routes has been accepted, and special inland transport rates are now offered to encourage manufacturers in Scotland and the North of England to send goods destined for Australia to Tilbury, where the Port of London Authority has built a major ocean terminal. Other ports that have container berths in operation include Felixstowe and Southampton, and many others, both large and small, have invested millions in container-berth facilities.

Although there has been a decline in the volume of conventional cargo handled by the large traditional ports (London, Liverpool, Manchester) there has been considerable growth at the smaller ports (like Dover, Felixstowe and Harwich), partly due to containerisation and the use of roll-on roll-off facilities. An additional factor has been that the smaller ports have had very few labour-relations problems. Offshore oil developments have had a substantial effect on port traffic by greatly increasing the flow through some northern ports, reducing oil traffic at traditional oil-importing terminals like Milford Haven.

Though the British merchant fleet, virtually all privately owned, has declined from its 1975 peak – due to the world recession in shipping and increasing international competition especially from ships operating under flags of convenience – it is still the fourth largest in the world (after Liberia, Japan and Greece). 94% of the

UK's overseas trade by weight (about three-quarters by value) is carried by sea.

Roll-on roll-off
'Roll-on roll-off' refers to the movement of vehicles by sea ferry, the vehicle being driven on and off the ferry. This method of transport was pioneered in the last war by troop and tank-carrying craft. In recent years the growth in this form of transport has been extremely rapid; ferries operate from Tilbury and other ports to Ireland and Europe.

Thus the roll-on roll-off concept brings Belfast barely a week away from Moscow. Goods can be loaded on to a lorry or container at the factory and driven straight through with no intermediate handling, and the minimum of customs' formalities. The vehicles carrying exports can be accompanied to their overseas markets by salesmen and technicians. Customers in Europe, one of the largest and most concentrated markets in the world, are no longer across the sea but just down the road.

Most vehicles travel under a TIR *(Transport Internationale Routier)* specification, which is an agreed specification to which vehicles must be built in order to pass through customs at frontiers without inspection. The range of goods carried includes chemicals, paper, textiles and general cargo.

Civil aviation

The government's role
The Civil Aviation Authority is an independent statutory body responsible for the general regulation of the industry, and it also provides air navigation services. The authority's main objective is to ensure that UK airlines provide adequate services to meet public demand at the lowest costs consistent with high safety standards. Funding of the authority's service is met by the government.

The UK has 150 civil airports (many very small), but the seven major ones handle over three-quarters of air passengers and air cargo traffic. These seven airports are owned by the British Airports Authority, a statutory body. British airports handle almost 60 million passengers a year, nearly half of these at Heathrow, the world's busiest airport for international travel.

The reason for London's predominance in international air travel stems from the capital's role as a world business, financial and tourist centre, and as the largest centre of population of an industrial country that is heavily dependent on overseas trade.

Air transport is an attractive means of moving high-value goods swiftly and safely, and it is not surprising that air cargo has been increasing at a fast rate during the last decade. About 20% of imports and exports (by value) are now carried by air. Among the exports are machinery, clothing, medicinal products and diamonds.

British Airways, in terms of international passengers and passenger-kilometres flown, is the largest airline in the world. Plans of the 1979 Conservative government included changing British Airways from a nationalised industry to a private sector company (see page 38), selling off a large minority of its shares to the public. The implementation of the plans depends on which government is in power after the next election.

There are a number of independent airlines operating – the largest is British Caledonian Airways with 30 aircraft; most of their operations are charter flights. Helicopters operate on a comparatively small scale, being mainly employed on offshore oil and gas activities. There is also a small amount of domestic air traffic, mainly passenger flights to and from Scotland, as well as an increasing amount of mail movement for the Post Office.

Pipelines

An interesting development has been the rapid extension of pipelines, a form of transport with natural characteristics. Its advantages are that it provides for a continuous movement of commodities in bulk, dispensing with the moving vehicle, and is very economical in utilisation of space. Disadvantages are that it is geographically inflexible, and relatively inflexible in its ability to carry a variety of commodities.

Oil pipelines brought ashore nearly 90% of offshore oil in 1981. There exists already over 750 miles (1200 km) of submarine pipeline for this purpose; additionally onshore ore pipelines carry refined products to major marketing areas (e.g. one pipeline runs from Milford Haven to Manchester, a distance of 300 miles [500 km]). There is also a national high-pressure pipeline system of some 3500 miles (5600 km) for the distribution of natural gas.

Problems of road and rail transport

With 16 million private cars on the road in the UK there seems no prospect of putting public transport on an economically viable basis even though the 1968 Transport Act did reduce the financial obligations of the railways. At present the railways in terms of passenger-miles carry only 7% of total traffic, but receive £1 billion annual subsidy (about £20 per head).

The chief burden of the railways lies in the heavy fixed or indirect costs of maintaining the track, signalling and stations, and in the extra costs of imposing adequate safety regulations – which does not apply to anything like the same extent to private and public road transport.

The successful financial viability of the railways would seem to lie in the area of such routes as the Inter-City services, from 'the heart of one city to another'. The Inter-City 125 services, operated by high speed trains (HST), have been very successful in terms of revenue-earning.

One problem, particularly applicable to public road and rail transport, is lack of utilisation of resources: it is only during rush hours that vehicles are fully used. Road passenger transport is a labour-intensive industry, and labour charges are constant whether a bus is empty or full. A state of cross-subsidisation exists: routes in rural areas which do not pay because of lack of passengers are subsidised by urban or suburban routes which themselves in recent years have showed little profit, with the resultant evaporation of profit and funds necessary for capital replacement at current cost. Thus many private bus companies need infusion of new capital to replace ageing buses, and this is the reason for the provisions in the 1968 Act for the formation of a National Bus Company and Passenger Transport Authority. However, it must be pointed out that the experience of the Massachusetts Bay Transportation Authority (said to be a carbon copy of the PTAs) is not particularly encouraging and has been described by the local American press as a 'sprawling deficit-ridden system'.

In the public sector 17000 vehicles are operated by the National Bus Company and another 25000 by other public authorities (e.g. London Transport). In addition there are 5000 private firms running an average of five vehicles each, but few are involved with scheduled services. Almost 80 trams still operate in Blackpool and Llandudno, the UK's only remaining tramway systems!

Because of the growth of the private car there has been a long-term decline in the use of public bus and coach services; between 1970 and 1980 a drop of 20% occurred. Steps taken to attempt to deal with the situation have included the large-scale introduction of 'one-man' vehicles, and in rural areas the introduction of 'post-bus' services. Withdrawal of uneconomic rural services may have reduced financial losses but has, in many cases, eliminated bus transport in rural areas.

Urban transport

The basic problem is congestion resulting from the ever-growing number and increased use of private cars. Possible solutions to the problem are:

(a) Traffic engineering, such as one-way streets and parking meters.

(b) Expansion of urban roads, though the cost is thought to be prohibitive and would cause tremendous social inconvenience, such as destruction of houses and shops.

(c) Restraint – parking charges are a simple form of such restraint. A 'toll' on cars entering the central areas of London and other big cities is another method, but this would delay traffic at entry points.

(d) A more sophisticated attempt at rationing would be the 'black box' or some other means of charging for the actual use of the roads. Both this system and the 'toll' method would be strongly resented by the motoring community. The problem with road pricing is to devise a system that is both sensible and practical, and ensures the optimum flow of traffic on the roads.

Structure of the road haulage industry

Road haulage is largely an industry of small businesses. There are 120000 operators with an average fleet size of four vehicles. The largest operator is the National Freight Company, which has recently been 'privatised' (see Chapter 4). Under the 1968 Transport Act a new licensing system was introduced, mainly affecting heavy lorries on long distance work: the rules relate to matters like having adequate financial and technical resources and control of the drivers' working conditions. Common Market requirements must now also be observed.

Recent changes in transport control

The 1980 and 1981 Transport Acts include measures to increase competition in the public-owned transport field in the UK. Many of the restrictions imposed on passenger road transport have been relaxed. The result has been a great increase in express coach services on some popular routes, with fare reductions. This may affect services in other areas adversely.

British Rail are in the process of divesting themselves of some of their non-railway subsidiary businesses, including hotels and hovercraft services.

Finally, arrangements are on hand to introduce private capital into the National Bus Company.

The future

There are many problems that need solving. Some of the major considerations are:

1   The Serpell Report: in January 1983 this report set out various options for British Rail, including several which would involve drastic pruning of many rail services.
2   To consider the extent to which subsidies should be paid to transport undertakings.
3   The increasing traffic congestion in urban areas.
4   The cross-Channel link: some eight proposals, varying from bridges to bored tunnels, including one for a single-track rail-only tunnel, are currently being considered by the government.
5   The increasing risk of collision at sea by super-tankers, and the pollution of sea and beaches. International agreement has been reached to deal with the pollution problem, but total enforcement may well be difficult.
6   The problem of jet aircraft noise. As far as subsonic jet aircraft are concerned, a certificate of quietness is now required by aircraft using British airports. The noise standards follow the recommendations of the 1969 Montreal conference of the International Civil Aviation Organisation. There are various noise abatement measures in force at some airports (e.g. limitations on night landings or take-offs).

13

Insurance

'By means of which policies of insurance . . . the loss lighteth rather easily upon many, than heavily on few.' This extract from an Act of Parliament dated 1601 probably shows more clearly than any definition since attempted the purpose of insurance.[1] Its basic function is the spreading of risk. The insured (the 'many') regularly contribute agreed sums (premiums), based on the degree of danger present, into a common fund, from which those who suffer the misfortune insured against (the 'few') draw compensation; the fortunate subsidise the unfortunate. The insurer assesses the premiums payable in the light of past experience and estimated future claims, and hopes that he will make a profit. If he is unwise and reckless his business will eventually fail, though it will probably last longer than a firm dealing in goods, because the insurer sells future protection for which he receives payment in advance.

Everybody and every business organisation takes risks and chances daily. The private citizen puts himself (and others) at risk every time he drives his car on the public highway; he takes a chance when he changes jobs. The businessman may find that goods have been stolen from his warehouse; he may make a trading loss due to an unwise purchase of stock. The burden of many, but not all, risks can be transferred to an insurer, thus freeing the insured from some categories of worry. Generally, a risk is only insurable if it is possible to estimate in the aggregate the likelihood of its occurrence. It is not possible to say whether any particular property will be

[1]In this chapter the common British practice of using 'insurance', 'insurer' and 'insured' will be followed, except when referring to life assurance.

damaged by fire, but it is possible to forecast, reasonably accurately, the total likely loss in a given period. Furthermore, an estimate can be made of the likely overall damage to a particular type of property in a certain area.

The law of averages works very well with large numbers, and it is in the interest of the insurer to have as many transactions on his books as possible. If he secures 20000 clients there is more likelihood of the law of averages applying than if he has only 2000 (try spinning a coin 10 times, then 100 times); again, the more normal, or better than normal, risks he underwrites (insurance term for the acceptance of risks and assessment of terms) the better.

Uninsurable risks

Generally these are risks that are not measurable, owing to insufficient information being available to the insurer to enable him to calculate the premium. So trade risks (e.g. a loss due to change in fashion) are normally uninsurable. Reference has already been made to the risk taken by an individual changing jobs; it would be quite impossible for an insurer to calculate the mathematical possibility of the person concerned suffering a loss in income and prospects if he has made an unwise decision.

A contract with an unlawful aim is invalid; nor are risks insurable if they are not in the public interest.

History of insurance

Insurance in some form existed in pre-Christian times. Four thousand years ago the trader carrying goods from Babylon to countries overseas was protected by a form of insurance that freed him from responsibility if the goods were lost en route through no fault of his own; as the usual commercial practice was for the trader to pledge his life and the lives of his family as security for the goods, the insurance was a true 'life-saver'. The Phoenicians, Indians, Greeks and Romans all practised some form of mercantile insurance; bottomry bonds were issued, under which loans were made against the security of the ship if the captain was unable to meet expenses at a foreign port – the loan was not repayable if the ship sank. It is interesting to note that in AD 529 interest was fixed at 1%

per month. Hundreds of years earlier, life assurance had begun to be practised in Rome and in countries under Roman rule. One interesting form of assurance available provided compensation to the husband if his wife died, because the marriage dowry then had to be returned to his father-in-law.

The earliest marine policy referring to this country is dated 20 September 1547, a fourteen-line document relating to a voyage from Cadiz to London. Chambers of Assurance were opened in London in 1575 to settle marine insurance disputes, and the first statute relating to marine insurance became law in 1601 (reference has already been made to this Act). In 1680 Edward Lloyd opened his coffee house in the City where individual merchants who underwrote marine risks met ship-owners, merchants and sea captains. Two companies – the London Assurance and the Royal Exchange Assurance – were granted Royal Charters in 1720 in return for cash payments to the government of £300 000 each. They were granted monopoly powers over all other companies, but individual underwriters remained unfettered.

Fire insurance began, for all practical purposes, after the Great Fire of 1666. One Nicholas Barden, a builder, set up office as a fire insurer about 1680 and wisely charged double premiums for timber houses, compared with brick ones. In the next 100 years many fire offices and friendly socieities were founded, and gradually they began to cover risks other than fire.

The earliest recorded life assurance in this country was in 1583, but unfortunately for the sixteen underwriters concerned, William Gibbon, whose life was assured, died eleven months after the one-year contract was arranged. Life assurance in its present form of a permanent contract renewed annually at the option of the policy holder dates from 1762, when the Equitable Life Assurance Society, formed in that year, first used mortality tables to calculate premiums. At first, life offices confined themselves to life assurance only, but later companies began to transact both life and fire business.

The real impetus to the growth of mercantile insurance came with the Industrial Revolution: rapid development of insurance of all forms to meet the ever-growing needs of industry became the order of the day. Personal accident insurance became popular among persons undertaking venturesome railway journeys; and later in the nineteenth century employers began to seek cover against claims by workmen or their relatives for compensation for injuries or death arising from accidents in the course of employment. With greater prosperity a demand for burglary insurance developed. The production of the internal combustion engine at the beginning of this century provided an enormous stimulus to the insurance business. The First World War caused another great increase in property values and immense new enterprises started. In the post-1920 era, although there was a worldwide recession, mass production of the motor car made motor insurance extremely important, and in the last twenty-five years the developments in the aviation, electronic and nuclear-power industries have again widened and increased the scope of insurance business.

The modern world could not carry on without the protection afforded by insurance. Industrialisation of our society has brought about an enormous increase in the accumulation of capital, and the owner of that capital need not risk it unnecessarily without insurance protection.

Principles of insurance

To ensure that insurance is not employed for purposes of speculation, insurance practice is subject to several legal principles, described as the principles of insurable interest, utmost good faith, indemnity and proximate cause. Each of these will now be considered in some detail.

Insurable interest
This has been defined by an authority on insurance law (E. J. Macgillivray) as follows:

> 'where . . . the happening of the event on which the insurance premium is . . . payable would involve the assured in the loss . . . of any right recognised by law or in any legal liability . . . there is an insurable interest . . .'

The principle was established by the Life Assurance Act 1774 and the Gaming Act 1845. Without insurable interest a contract becomes a wager and is not enforceable. A can insure his own car against damage, but cannot so insure B's car, in which he has no interest. It should be noted that a husband and wife have an unlimited insurable interest in each other's life, and a creditor has an interest in the life of his debtor. Before 1774 the placing of insurance on the lives of public men was common, and 'having something' on the life of the Prince of Wales was not unusual.

Except for life and marine insurance the insurable interest must exist throughout the duration of the contract. In life assurance, since the majority of policies have a cash value after they have been in force for some while, the policy holder must be free to transfer the benefit as with any other form of security; so the insurable interest need only exist at the time the policy is effected. In marine cargo insurance, as ownership needs to be freely transferable while cargo is en route, it is necessary for the insurance cover to be similarly transferable.

Utmost good faith

Although the general rule at common law is *caveat emptor* (let the buyer beware), nevertheless in certain types of contracts – and insurance is one – the principle of utmost good faith, or *uberrima fides*, operates. The parties to the contract must deal openly and honestly with each other and disclose all material facts: that is, any fact that might influence a prudent insurer in his decision whether or not to accept a particular risk or to charge a certain rate of premium. This responsibility bears largely on the proposer because the insurer has to make the commercial decision whether to underwrite the risk, based mainly on the information provided by the proposer. The latter is asked to complete a proposal form with a signed declaration that he has given true answers and disclosed all material facts. This duty continues up to the time the contract is made. In a well-known legal case the insurers were held to be not liable, because the proposer did not disclose at the time his proposal was accepted that he had contracted a serious illness, though when he filled in the form he had not yet become ill. But in the case of permanent contracts, such as life assurance, the insured is not bound to disclose any change in circumstances when he applies for renewal annually.

In practice, many insurance companies do not adhere too rigidly to the letter of the law in dealing with claims and are not likely to try to avoid payment on a technical inaccuracy. Thus, a lady who, in her vanity, stated she was 5 ft 5 in (162 cm), when her actual height was 5 ft 2 in (155 cm), would hardly be penalised when making a claim on a personal accident and sickness policy. But a car owner who had made basic engineering alterations to his vehicle to improve performance without disclosing this might find the insurer unsympathetic when he made a claim.

For his part, the insurer must disclose the exact terms of the contract. Criticism is sometimes made that some insurers are not keen to supply a specimen contract in advance to the prospective client, merely sending him a proposal form and outline information of the terms.

Indemnity

The object of this principle is to ensure that the insured who makes a valid claim should be fully, but not more than fully, compensated for the loss incurred; he should not make a profit out of his misfortune, because an unprincipled person might then consider 'staging' the event insured against. The principle cannot, of course, apply to life and personal accident policies because injury or loss of life can hardly be given a money value – this latter type of policy is a 'benefit' policy, with fixed predetermined sums paid when a valid claim is made.

In practice, many problems arise in trying to apply the principle of indemnity accurately. It is difficult to estimate the amount of depreciation on a car. In times of inflation and shortage the value of certain items is likely to increase. If a 1969 car is stolen, then the insurer should pay such sum as would enable the policy holder to buy a similar model in the open market. A freehold house bought for £3500 in 1960 may well have been worth £30000 in 1983. In the event of total loss the insured will only be compensated in full if he has paid the premium based on the higher value. Other examples will readily come to the mind of the reader.

Two additional principles known as *subrogation* and *contribution* arise out of the basic one of indemnity. An example of subrogation occurs in a case where the insured has a legal right to recover from another person as well as claim under his own insurance policy. Assume that a householder who has insured the contents of his home loses a suitcase while in a hotel. It may well be that he will have a right of claim against the proprietor. The insurer takes over the householder's rights against the hotel immediately, so that he will be paid only once for the loss. If the hotel accepts liability and pays the insurer the value of the lost case, then the latter will not be out of pocket at all. Similarly, under the principle of contribution, if two insurances are effected on the same property (and there is nothing illegal about this) the insured cannot claim compensation twice; in practice, he claims against both companies and receives a proportionate payment from each.

Proximate cause

This can best be explained by a practical example. If a fire occurs in a property, then damage may be caused not only by the flames themselves but also by the efforts made to extinguish the fire. A valid claim could be made for compensation for all the damage, because that caused by water from the firemen's hoses was a direct or proximate result of the peril covered by the contract. The loss must come about from an uninterrupted chain of happenings set into movement by the occurrence of the event actually covered by the contract. In practice, considerable difficulty may be experienced in determining whether a claim is valid, and this may well have to be decided by the courts.

Organisation of British insurance

The sellers of insurance can be divided into several groups, and each will now be considered. The majority of the institutions mentioned are members of the British Insurance Association or the Life Offices Association, both of which exist to maintain high standards in the industry.

Industrial Life (or Home Service) Assurance Companies and Friendly Societies

The insurers employ agents who call at the homes of policy holders selling 'home service' life assurance – the term has replaced the older one 'industrial'. Premiums are collected by the agent at weekly or monthly intervals on a commission basis. The sum assured on any one policy is limited. The volume of this type of assurance has decreased in recent years, though in the less affluent years in the decades before the last world war the vast majority of private policy holders in the country used the services provided by insurance agents. Over 100 million industrial life policies are still in force and most offices use their agency network to obtain other business. Most offices that started as industrial life now only underwrite ordinary life and general insurance business.

The companies

Some of these are proprietary, that is profit-making, companies with shareholders. Others are mutual offices, that is the policy holders are the members and there is no share capital provided by shareholders. It does not follow that the latter charge lower premiums than the former; as in other fields of business, there are many factors that determine prices and no useful generalisations can be made.

The Insurance Companies Acts and the Companies Acts make certain provisions in an attempt to protect the public from companies with inadequate financial resources.

Lloyd's

This is best regarded as an insurance exchange resembling in some ways the Stock Exchange. It is a corporation, regulated by a series of special Acts of Parliament (a new one is expected to be enacted in 1983) and governed by its own committee. It provides facilities for individual underwriters to transact business. An underwriter, who is normally a member of a *syndicate* (a group of persons who share risks in certain agreed proportions), has to satisfy stringent minimum conditions, particularly financial, laid down by the committee. Each underwriter has unlimited personal liability to the full extent of his insurance commitments, and other syndicate members are under no obligation to make good a deficiency. However, a fund maintained by compulsory contributions from all underwriters ensures that no policy holder suffers in the event of the insolvency of any one member.

Syndicates may vary from a few to several hundred members, but only a small proportion of them actually practise – underwriting agents or salaried officials transact the business on behalf of the group. About one fifth of all British premium income is earned by Lloyd's underwriters, of whom there are over 19 000 grouped into 420 syndicates.

The public can deal only through a Lloyd's broker (of whom there are over 200); he may well approach several leading underwriters in the underwriting room for competitive quotations before a rate is agreed. In many cases, several syndicates will each accept a proportion of the risk at the same rate per cent as the *leader*. A typical current motor policy shows that the risk is covered by six syndicates, totalling 140 members; the leader, with about 80 members, has accepted 73% of the risk, each individual member of this syndicate taking between ½% and 2%.

The Lloyd's broker is responsible for preparing the policy; yearly over two million of them are channelled through the Lloyd's policy signing office, where the contracts are completed. Rather less than half the total business transacted at Lloyd's is now connected with shipping.

Other intermediaries in insurance

Mention has already been made of industrial life assurance agents and Lloyd's brokers, both of whom receive commission for their services from the insurer. Similarly, there are two other categories of intermediaries who obtain and place business with companies. They are:

1   Insurance brokers (non-Lloyd's). These are full-time specialists, generally with their own offices, who advise the public and place business in the best part of the market. Many of them have agencies with a large number of companies and may also handle claims for their clients. Under a recent Act insurance brokers (both Lloyd's and non-Lloyd's) are controlled by a registration council.

2   Insurance agents. These perform the same function as brokers. Generally they operate on a part-time basis and are in a position to introduce business to companies because they are in a trade or profession that puts them in touch with persons likely to need insurance advice. Bank managers, accountants and garage owners often have agencies for this reason. The agent is unlikely to have contacts with more than one or two companies.

Re-insurance

This refers to the arrangement by which an insurer agrees to accept, normally in bulk, a portion of the risks already taken by another insurer. It is often called *indirect* business, and the responsibility of the primary insurer who transacted the *direct* business with the client is in no way affected by the re-insurance. It might well be compared to the action of the bookmaker, who, having taken numerous bets on one horse, himself 'lays-off' a proportion of the amount staked with another bookmaker.

British insurance overseas

The British insurance market handles a very considerable proportion of overseas business, the largest single market being the USA, where much goodwill was created at the time of the San Francisco earthquake in 1906. Despite claims amounting to well over £500 million at modern values, British insurers met the liability in full. More than one half of the fire, accident and marine business of British companies is in respect of overseas countries. The premiums thus earned represent invisible exports to the UK (see page 163).

In accordance with the Treaty of Rome (see Chapter 14) directives are in force on various insurance matters with the intention of providing a 'common market', thus avoiding distortion of competition. These directives have been, or are being, implemented in UK legislation.

The insurance ombudsman

A number of leading insurance companies have established an insurance ombudsman bureau, supervised by an independent council, to deal with complaints by insured persons. The ombudsman has power to make very substantial cash awards in appropriate cases. Member companies are bound to accept his decision, though a claimant need not – in which case the latter can take legal action if desired.

The main types of insurance policies

Fire insurance
UK fire losses are currently over £300 million yearly, and therefore companies try to work closely with industrial owners at the design

stage to advise and suggest precautions. In the case of existing buildings, insurers often insist on the installation of sprinklers, fire doors and so forth before accepting a risk. It is usual for businesses to insure also against loss of profits consequent upon fire – income is likely to drop for a considerable period as a result of the dislocation of business after a fire, but heavy overhead expenses (e.g. rent, rates, salaries) will still have to be paid.

Cover against floods, storms and tempests is usually included in a fire insurance policy, and householders' comprehensive buildings and contents insurance will also include theft and claims by third parties (e.g. a visiting service engineer injured through the house-holder's negligence).

Accident insurance

In this field there is virtually nothing that cannot be insured. The term accident insurance is used generally to cover all categories other than fire, marine and life. Some of the main types of policy are dealt with below.

Employers' liability. Although for several decades the National Insurance scheme has included industrial injuries benefit, neverthe-less the employer is still likely to be sued for damages (if there has been negligence) even if the accident arises from using defective equipment which is the fault of the supplier. Since 1972 employers have had to effect compulsory insurance to cover their liability. The rate of insurance charged will naturally vary with the hazards of the particular trade.

Motor vehicles. Introduced compulsorily in 1930, this compels every driver of a motor vehicle to insure against claims arising from death or injury to any person (including his own passengers) caused by his vehicle being on the road. In practice, most vehicle owners have either full third party policies, thus also covering damage to the property of others, or comprehensive insurance, which additionally insures the driver, the insured vehicle and often its contents – this sort of policy is advisable because it ensures that compensation is received even if it is impossible to prove that the accident was the fault of another. The basis of charging the premium varies from insurer to insurer, but most assess the risk on the size and value of the vehicle, and the area of the country it is normally in, with rebates for 'no claims' years and other factors, and premium loadings for certain types of uses.

Dishonesty. It is possible to obtain cover for loss or damage caused by intruders, or resulting from the theft of items in transit or from the action of dishonest employees *(fidelity guarantee)*. In practice, theft of various kinds is often included in household, commercial or motor vehicle comprehensive insurance. As with fire insurance, the insurer may insist that certain precautions are taken before the risk is accepted.

Public liability. Owners or occupiers of premises may well be held liable for damages as a result of persons legitimately on their premises suffering injury or death – for example, a client might fall on a slippery floor or a customer might suffer from food poisoning from contaminated food in a restaurant. Damages may often be high, and prudent businessmen insure accordingly. Note that under the doctrine of *vicarious liability* the employer is likely to be held liable for the negligent acts of his staff in the course of their employment.

Other accident policies. There are a host of other accident policies: bad debts insurance (more common in the export field where much of the business is transacted by the ECGD, dealt with in Chapter 14); professional indemnity, covering claims for loss caused by negligence of a doctor, solicitor, architect, and so on; personal accident and sickness insurance, covering loss of income during disability resulting from sickness or accident; holidaymakers' policies, protecting against theft of baggage, and illness, accident and cancellation costs.

The 'package' policy, which includes a considerable number of risks, is becoming increasingly popular; and an innovation in recent years has been 'over the counter' insurance, where standard policies are sold in a few minutes like many other commodities.

Marine and aviation insurance

This is a separate study in itself, and only a brief note on this subject can be included. Marine insurance is the oldest form of insurance and was introduced to this country by Italian merchants probably 600 years ago; from the time of Elizabeth I the people who offered insurance to sailors and merchants were called *underwriters*, because they wrote their names under the promise to pay for ships or cargoes lost at sea. Lloyd's is the largest insurer in the world in the marine and aviation field; nearly half their total premium income is in respect of marine and aviation risks, including a great deal of foreign business. Basically, there are four types of marine insurance:

(a)   *Hull* – covering damage or loss both to the insured vessel and to others involved in incidents.

(b)   *Cargo.*

(c)   *Freight* – i.e. the charge for carriage; this is often included in (b).

(d)   *Ship-owners liability* – which will cover claims caused by his own or his employee's negligence in, say, dealing with cargo. The doctrine of *vicarious liability* has been referred to above.

Although there are few total losses of ships or aircraft (perhaps 200 a year out of a total of probably 30000 vehicles), nevertheless there are a vast number of incidents causing partial losses or damage, generally to cargo or equipment – there may well be one claim for every three ships or aircraft.

Incidentally, Lloyd's provide the world with the most comprehensive shipping intelligence service available. An enormous volume of information is provided by 1500 Lloyd's agents throughout the world, by radio stations, ship-owners and other sources; all this is collated and distributed. Perhaps the best-known publications are *Lloyd's List* and *Lloyd's Shipping Index*, which list all ocean-going vessels and their latest known positions, as well as much general information.

Life assurance

Unlike the other forms of insurance already mentioned, life assurance does not indemnify (see page 147), but undertakes to pay. In order to discharge its contractual obligations as they fall due in the years ahead, it must build up and maintain adequate stocks of money or securities. This stock of money is its *common fund*, which is built up from premiums scientifically calculated to ensure that the fund will always be large enough to pay all benefits as they become due. Thus the distinctive feature of the fund is its *mutuality*, each policy holder possessing the right to draw agreed benefits as they become due. A life fund is a reservoir of money which, unlike water, is capable of earning more money; thus it is invested in a mixture of short- and long-term investments to ensure that, while earning dividends and interest as safely as possible, it is sufficiently 'liquid' to ensure that cash is available at the appropriate times to pay policy holders.

At fixed intervals every life office values its assets and liabilities (see Chapter 11) in the fund and distributes up to 90% of the actuarially calculated surplus to its policy holders who have *with profits* policies (they pay higher premium rates than *non-profits* insurers).

The Insurance Companies Acts lay down regulations for the protection of premium funds.

There are many forms of life policy. The main categories are:

(*a*) *Pure life:* payment is made only on the death of the person assured. Partner survivorship policies have already been referred to in Chapter 2. The business insures each partner so that if one dies and the business has to be wound up sufficient liquid funds are available to pay out to the estate of the deceased partner his appropriate share of the net assets.

(*b*) *Endowment:* payment is made at death or at the end of a fixed term of years, whichever is earlier. Naturally premium rates are higher than in (*a*).

(*c*) *Term:* under this type of cover, life assurance is granted for a fixed period only. A popular policy is *mortgage protection*. Another example arises where a person protects himself for a very short period, for example during an airline journey.

(*d*) *Annuity:* basically, in return for a fixed total premium, the insured receives an income (sometimes deferred) until death or other agreed date. Persons near retirement age often prefer to surrender a proportion of their capital in return for a fixed income until death.

Nowadays, many life insurers also sell pension schemes and unit trusts, including life assurance, property bonds, and so on.

Some idea of the size of the life assurance market can be gauged from the total life assurance funds of British companies; at present, this is about £40000 million (about £800 per head of population). A considerable proportion of this sum is invested by insurance companies in property and in securities. To encourage the public to make suitable provision for life assurance income tax concessions are made by the government.

Insurance money and influence

It has already been seen that British insurers are major investors; the distribution over different types of assets is as follows:

Mortgages & loans	10%	Property	12%
Central and local government securities	29%	Miscellaneous	11%
Stocks/shares/debentures in commercial enterprise	38%		

By reason of their investments, British insurance companies hold over 10% of all ordinary shares quoted on the Stock Exchange but rarely involve themselves in the management of the companies in which they invest. About one half of the non-life business is overseas and the insurance companies' annual contribution to Britain's invisible earnings (Chapter 14) is currently over £500 million.

The part played by insurance companies in the area of loss prevention has already been mentioned. British insurance has its own fire protection association, pays part of the cost of the fire research station, and produces films and printed material on safety and security matters. Perhaps its biggest contribution is in charging higher premiums to those who take little care and in reducing payments for those who install effective equipment for protection purposes.

14

Overseas Trade

The advantages of foreign trade

Much of our industrial and commercial activity is devoted to satisfying the population's daily needs. We cannot find all the necessary raw materials within these shores to carry this out and, similarly, we cannot produce even half the food needed for the population. But this does not explain why the United Kingdom buys from abroad vast quantities of primary commodities (raw materials), food and manufactured goods that we are capable of producing here – for example, greater quantities of wheat could be grown, more animals bred, more cash registers manufactured. The reasons why we do not do this are twofold: first, countries must 'live and let live' in their trading arrangements with others. If country A exports certain items to country B, B will need to export some of its products (either to A or to C); so to some extent A (or C) has to give consideration to the sort of items B wishes to dispose of. Secondly, it is considered, in general terms, to be in the interests of all if each country specialises in producing those goods and services it can best provide. This is called the *principle of comparative costs* and is merely an extension of division of labour.

There are several ways in which this operates. In some instances, only certain countries are capable of providing particular commodities, either because they have a suitable climate or because raw materials are found in their areas. Again, it may be that a certain type of item suits a particular operation – thus Canadian 'hard' wheat is better for making flour for bread, whereas British 'soft' wheat is more satisfactory for biscuit manufacture. Finally, one country may have acquired special skills which give them advantages over their rivals; thus Britain was one of the world's leading exporters of heavy manufactured capital goods (e.g. engines) until the Second World War and is now a very important producer of man-made fibres. In the field of services, British insurance and banking (both already referred to) have a worldwide reputation.

Ideally, genuine multilateral free trade would probably benefit the world more than a system of restrictive tariffs, taxes and duties. In practice, the principle of comparative cost is allowed to work only imperfectly. Defence, political and protectionist trade considerations may cause restrictions to be imposed – for example, the USA subsidised the manufacture of synthetic rubber during a period when natural rubber (at that time more satisfactory for most production purposes) could have been bought more cheaply from Malaya. Furthermore some countries, regretfully, whilst not actually controlling imports of certain goods, introduce regulations, sometimes of a somewhat petty nature, making it very difficult for firms attempting to sell goods to them.

The pattern of world trade

To give the reader a general picture of the world trading scene, the following chart shows details of the imports and exports of the countries which together are responsible for around 60% of all international trade.

The chart shows how the export scene is dominated by the USA and Germany, which together have greater total exports than the next four countries in descending order of magnitude. In fact the USA and Germany are now responsible for about 23% of the world's exports. Though the UK is still in the export premier division (lying in fifth place in 1980) it has suffered a great decline in ranking order, having been in second place but twenty years ago.

However, mere comparison of the value of foreign trade of different countries does not reveal the whole picture; it is important to consider the figures in relation to national income. Thus, for example, the USA spends only 10% of her national income on imports, the UK about a quarter, and Belgium just over one half. So a reduction of, say, 20% in imports by the USA would cause serious dislocation in world trade but make little difference in the country

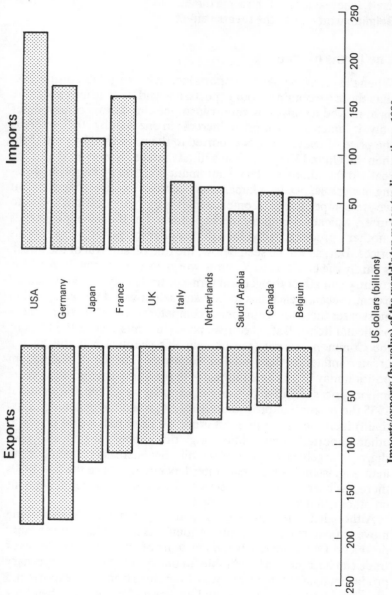

Exports

Imports

USA
Germany
Japan
France
UK
Italy
Netherlands
Saudi Arabia
Canada
Belgium

250   200   150   100   50   50   100   150   200   250

US dollars (billions)

Imports/exports (by value) of the world's ten major trading nations, 1980

itself, whereas a cut of the same dimension (in percentage terms) by Belgium would have the reverse effect.

The terms of trade

When the prices we pay for imports increase by a greater proportion than those we obtain for our exports, it is said that the terms of trade have moved against this country; so, looking at two commodities only, if Jamaican sugar prices increase in one year by 20%, whereas the price of television sets exported to them is raised by only 15%, then the United Kingdom is at a disadvantage. However, it must be realised that there will be no automatic solution by merely increasing our prices, because Jamaica will continue to buy from us only if we are competitive. To some extent it is the 'supplicant' who has to suffer, whichever country this happens to be. If one country needs another's products badly, then the supplier can possibly increase his prices. But, as will be seen below, the rule of 'survival of the fittest' is hardly the best way to promote world economic growth. Any one country can affect the general terms of trade only to a very limited extent (because each has to buy and sell in world markets, and in most cases there are a number of competing states able to produce a particular item). But, of course, powerful units such as the USA or the Common Market (see later in this chapter) will still have a greater influence than smaller countries. The United Kingdom position may be of some interest – in the immediate postwar years import prices, relative to those of exports, were high. From about 1955 the position improved until 1973/4, when the massive (unjustified) increase in the price of crude oil occurred; world prices of other imported commodities (e.g. tin, rubber, sugar) also rose sharply, largely as a result of the oil price increase (remember 'no man is an island' – we are all interdependent). Since the late 1970s there has been some improvement: the UK is no longer dependent on other countries for its oil supplies.

Although it is helpful to the United Kingdom if the terms of trade move in favour of manufacturing countries and against the primary producers (as has tended to happen quite often in the past), terms of trade can become too favourable for one party; thus if poor primary producers such as Ghana receive a low return from their exports and are compelled to pay relatively high prices for imports, then they will either try to manage without the latter or, if manufactured goods are the ones involved, attempt to make them themselves. Unfortunately for them, the capital equipment needed to do this has often to be imported, and anyway the technical knowledge is often lacking. Thus the poor countries may become poorer and international trade may be adversely affected. Incidentally, this trend in terms of trade in favour of the richer industrial countries will possibly reverse within the next thirty years, because increasing world population is likely to lead to food and raw material shortages.

International financial institutions

There is enormous inequality of income in the world. Although caution is necessary in interpolating comparative statistics of national incomes per head of population, nevertheless they clearly show the enormous differences in wealth.

Consider the following:

(a) Twenty countries (1978 figures) had average annual incomes *per head* of $5000 and above (Switzerland the highest with $12000, followed by Sweden, the USA and West Germany – with the UK near the bottom of the first division). At least fifty countries had incomes of $2000 and below, with half of them below $1000.

(b) Grouping countries together shows that the top twenty have an income per head of around fifty times the bottom twenty.

The vast gap between the rich and the poor countries is the main factor preventing the balanced growth of world trade, and it is also a grave danger to world peace. In our attempt to materially assist the underdeveloped countries and to encourage world trade, a number of institutions have been set up since 1944.

The World Bank

Established as a result of the Bretton Woods Agreement in 1944, its main function is to lend money to needy countries and to encourage private investment by granting guarantees as long as the money is used for productive purposes and not for developing social services, because it is the former that will give an immediate tangible gain and, incidentally, make it possible to repay the loan. There are now over 100 member countries, each subscribing capital according to its means. Like other banks, the World Bank receives and normally charges interest; though in recent years, through an affiliated organisation, loans have been made to less developed countries usually without interest. To date over 1000 million has been lent to countries like India, Italy and Japan.

The International Monetary Fund (IMF)

This was also set up as a result of Bretton Woods. Whereas the World Bank is concerned mainly with lending capital, the IMF's basic function is to encourage world trade by improving trade relations between countries. Hence it tries to ensure stable exchange rates and to discourage devaluation without consultation. It also provides short-term credit for countries with temporary balance-of-payments difficulties; the United Kingdom was a very large borrower in 1968. Each of the member countries provides a quota based on its currency and gold situation. The IMF has had some considerable measure of success; but one difficulty has been that, while its powerful member countries will accept certain basic principles for conducting world-trade finances, not all members have been keen to have the principles applied to them in practice.

General Agreement on Tariff and Trade (GATT)

This treaty came into operation in 1948. There are about 140 members, and the general aim is to reduce existing trade restrictions. Basically, member countries agree not to show trading discrimination against each other, to consult when tariff changes are contemplated and to work towards a general reduction in tariff barriers. As with the IMF, GATT has proved partly successful in achieving its aims; for example, as a result of the Kennedy round of talks in 1967, agreement was reached by over fifty countries to reduce over a period of years tariffs on industrial goods by around 30%. The Tokyo round of goods, which took four years to complete, further reduced tariffs. However, as briefly mentioned earlier in this chapter, the growth of what are called non-tariff barriers (complicated administrative procedures, health and safety regulations, etc.), though often quite genuine, have been used by some countries to limit imports.

Balance of trade and balance of payments

Imports and exports can be divided into two groups:

1   *Visible* – that is, actual goods one country buys from another.
2   *Invisible* – foreign currency earned or spent in selling or buying services. Some of these have been referred to in previous chapters. The UK's main invisible exports are:
    (*a*)   Services provided by UK banks and other financial and trading institutions, and interest, profits and dividends from investments abroad.
    (*b*)   Insurance placed in the UK market by foreigners.
    (*c*)   Freight earnings arising from foreigners using British ships and aircraft.
    (*d*)   Receipts from foreign tourists to the UK (where they spend their own currencies).
    (*e*)   British films and records sold abroad (and, incidentally, the earnings of UK entertainers abroad).
    (*f*)   Re-exports. Various countries pay for services to commodities. For example, crude oil is imported purely to be refined and re-exported.

The UK's invisible imports are the reverse of the above items (*a*) to (*f*) – for example, British firms using foreign transport; or the expenditure abroad of UK residents on holiday. In fact, invisible imports in respect of the reversal of items (*b*) and (*f*) are not substantial. Government expenditure overseas (diplomatic, military and aid to developing countries) also counts as invisible imports, as does the UK's net payment to the Common Market (see later in this chapter). Generally the UK has earned a surplus from its invisible transactions. In 1980 this was £2000 million (in 1979 it was £2600 million). The net earnings of the UK from invisibles is second only to those of the USA. When only visibles are counted, the term *balance of trade* is used, whilst the whole account is called the *balance of payments*.

The United Kingdom has generally had a deficit of balance of trade (crude trade gap) for the whole of this century, but in the years up to the Second World War a large invisible surplus redressed the balance. As a result of selling foreign investments (e.g. Argentine

Railways) to finance the war, the position has changed materially and there have been periodic balance-of-payments crises.

Except for a few years immediately after the Second World War, there has always been a surplus on 'invisibles', though very much smaller than pre-1939, and it is not always realised that since 1949, taking the whole balance-of-payments position into account, there have been almost as many favourable as unfavourable years. It is worth noting that the UK had a visible trade surplus in 1971, but since then has not been in surplus until 1980 and 1981. The rise in the oil price during 1979 materially contributed to this situation, but its downward plunge in the early 1980s is likely to adversely affect the situation again.

The commodity composition of our overseas trade

In total value UK export of goods in 1980 amounted to £47 000 million (say £900 per head) and imports were about 2% less. In terms of volume, exports rose in that year by 2%, whilst imports fell by 5% (the latter figure reflects 'destocking' by businesses due to the reduction of economic activity in the UK).

The main reductions in imports in recent years have been in foodstuffs, resulting from the expansion of domestic agricultural production, and in basic commodities, due to the growing use of synthetic materials to replace such imported natural materials as rubber, wool and cotton. In contrast, imports of finished and semi-manufactures, particularly capital goods and industrial components, have increased considerably, partly because the countries producing the basic materials have tended to embark (often with help from the richer countries) upon the subsequent stages of manufacture themselves. The fourfold increase in oil prices in 1973/4 was responsible for a large increase in the value of fuel imports, but with North Sea oil becoming available the UK moved into self-sufficiency in the early 1980s and became an oil exporter.

The changing pattern of trade since 1960 is shown by the diagram illustrating the commodity composition of trade.

Geographical distribution of trade

Around three-quarters of Britain's exports and imports are with other developed countries. The major change in the last thirty years has been that Britain's trade with the rest of Western Europe has

Commodity composition of trade

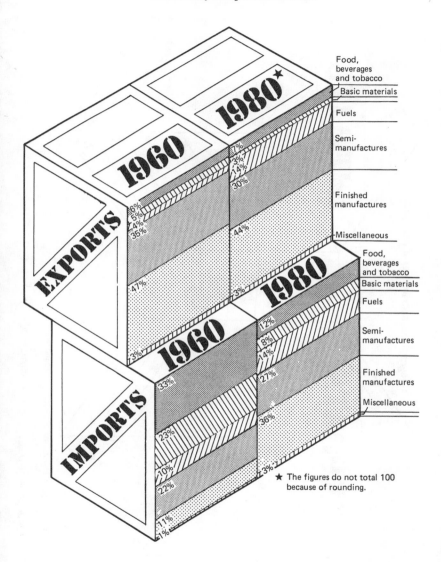

Reproduced by permission of the Controller of H.M. Stationery Office

Geographical distribution of trade, 1980

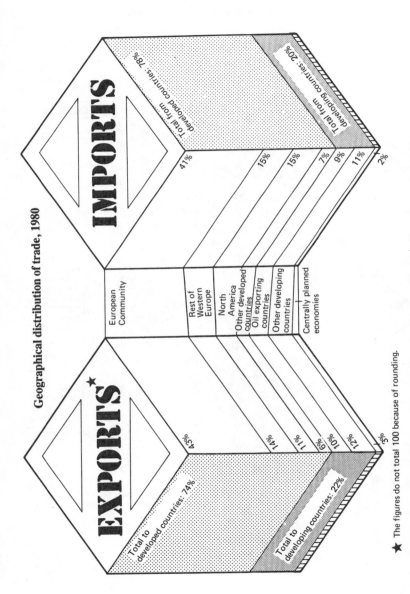

IMPORTS

Total from developed countries: 78%

Total from developing countries: 20%

41%

15%

15%

7%

9%

11%

2%

European Community

Rest of Western Europe

North America

Other developed countries

Oil exporting countries

Other developing countries

Centrally planned economies

EXPORTS ★

Total to developed countries: 74%

Total to developing countries: 22%

43%

14%

11%

6%

10%

12%

3%

★ The figures do not total 100 because of rounding.

Reproduced by permission of the Controller of H.M. Stationery Office become increasingly important: in 1950 it represented 30% of Britain's total trade, whereas in 1980 it was almost double that figure. European Community countries account for six of the top ten export markets and for six of the ten leading suppliers of goods to Britain. The Federal Republic of Germany is Britain's largest single export market, with the USA a close second; on the import side the position is reversed. The diagram shows the UK's exports by destination and imports by origin for 1980.

Conduct of the export trade

The methods of trading vary very considerably according to the firm, the industry, the product and the foreign market. Many exporters, particularly the smaller firms, use the services of specialist export merchants; some, however, sell to importers and consumers abroad through their own agents or resident representatives in the particular country concerned; others sell through their own branch offices or subsidiary companies in foreign countries.

There are now very few restrictions imposed by Britain on the movements of goods and services. The few controls in operation deal mainly with exports of items of strategic importance; special arrangements also exist in respect of Common Agricultural Policy products (see below).

Government assistance to overseas trade

Because of the vital importance of increasing Britain's exports, successive British governments have assisted exporters by trying to create conditions favourable to the export trade; thus credit-insurance facilities are provided, together with information and advice about export opportunities. Exporters needing help can apply to the offices of the British Overseas Trade Board (BOTB), which operates under the general authority of the Secretary of State for Trade and includes among its members representatives of commerce and industry as well as the Trades Union Congress (see Chapter 4). Through the board's channels there is access to the commercial posts of the diplomatic service overseas – there are 200 such posts, which supply information of every kind affecting trade with their territories. These overseas offices supply regular reports on local economic and commercial conditions, and in particular assist the exporter to overcome difficulties that may arise out of the government regulations of the importing country. Thus the BOTB can provide information about any country with reference to export problems, such as the commercial standing of foreign firms.

Many exhibitions and trade fairs are held which provide an important means of advertising and selling British goods. Participation in such fairs, 'British weeks' and store promotions overseas are an area of export promotion for which the government provides assistance.

Export credit insurance

Although all sellers giving credit take a certain risk of incurring bad debts, there are greater risks in dealing with overseas buyers: it is harder to assess credit-worthiness; rate of exchange variations may occur; overseas government regulations imposed after a contract is made may prevent receipt of payment; and political changes, particularly in the newly independent countries, may frustrate contracts.

The Export Credits Guarantee Department (ECGD), responsible to the Secretary of State for Trade (Chapter 15), provides protection to exporters, merchants, investors and banks against overseas credit risks by providing insurance cover against the main risks of not receiving payment; by guarantees to banks financing export trade which provide an acceptable security; and by insurance covering new investments against risks of expropriation, war, and so on. The department is self-supporting, charges premiums based on the risk involved and provides credit insurance for much of the external trade of British firms. It is true to say that, without the help of the ECGD, exporting would be far more hazardous than it is and the volume of trade would be very considerably less. About one third of our exports are covered by ECGD credit insurance. Investment insurance is provided for new British investment overseas against nationalisation, war damage and restrictions on remittances of profits to the UK.

Non-government aid to exporters

The work of the joint-stock and some of the merchant banks in the field of export is of considerable importance. In particular, much of the financial work in connection with payments between exporters and importers is handled by them. The banks maintain specialist export departments to give the businessman advice on conditions abroad and assistance in finding suitable markets and in carrying out the necessary documentation involved.

Considerable assitance to exporters is also given by chambers of commerce. These are voluntary bodies on which both large and small businesses are represented; they act as a storehouse of information on a wide range of subjects and maintain close links with the Department of Trade and Industry and the BOTB, pressing for government action whenever they feel that the interests of British exporters are being adversely affected.

In many industries trade associations have been set up to help member firms, and national associations such as the Confederation of British Industries are also able to offer considerable assistance to exporters and would-be exporters.

Financing of international trade

The exporter, obviously, will prefer to retain control over his goods until he is certain of payment. Payment by cheque against the document of title would not guarantee this since the cheque might not be met. So a variety of suitable methods exist, all of which use the banks as intermediaries. The documentary credit system is commonly used, whereby the importer's bank advises the exporter that a credit has been opened in his favour at the British bank. The exporter will be able to draw on this credit after goods have been despatched and the necessary documentation dealt with.

The appropriate documents will be sent by airmail to the importer's bank, and they will include a bill of lading (the legal title to the goods showing that they have been shipped). The British bank will be authorised to release funds to the exporter when the bill of lading has been received abroad. In other cases, if the buyer wishes to have credit facilities, the exporter will draw up a bill of exchange (Chapter 8), which, after acceptance by the buyer, can be discounted with a financial institution by the exporter; thus the exporter receives immediate cash and the buyer abroad does not pay until the bill matures. It should be realised that this system can operate only if the buyer has a satisfactory credit status, for otherwise his signature of acceptance on the bill would be worthless. This is one of the areas where using the services of the BOTB can be a great advantage; it is able to supply information about the buyer, and the premiums for credit insurance depend to some extent on the buyer's status. Exporters who have taken out ECGD policies are able to borrow from banks on favourable terms comparatively easily, and, of course, acceptance houses and discount houses (Chapter 8) will the more readily be prepared to add their names to bills (thus taking over responsibility for payment) or to discount them, as required.

The commodity markets

Britain is still the major international centre for transactions in a vast range of commodities. Many of the sales in these markets refer to goods that will never actually be landed on British soil. Thus these markets, which have often been established here for centuries, not only cater for the import of goods for home use but also earn very valuable amounts of foreign currency by invisible exports (see page 163). Among the important markets are the Baltic Exchange (shipping and air transport), the London Commodity Exchange (cocoa, coffee, rubber, sugar etc.) and the Metal Exchange. In some markets an important aspect of the work is that in *futures*: that is, commodities may be quoted for delivery some months ahead at a price agreed now. For some commodities the markets quote a number of prices, varying according to delivery date. Although much future dealing involves food manufacturers trying to ensure a regular supply of a commodity, there is also some speculative dealing in this area (as there is on the Stock Exchange, Chapter 3). In most of the markets the commodities can be very accurately graded and described, and it is because of this that dealing can take place without an actual inspection of the goods being necessary.

The Foreign Exchange Market

The market consists of around 200 authorised banks and a number of firms of foreign-exchange brokers acting as intermediaries between the banks. They deal with the commodity of money, thus providing those engaged in international trade with the necessary foreign currencies. They buy and sell for both spot (i.e. immediate) and future (or forward) delivery. This forward market enables businesses that, at a fixed date in the future, are due to receive or make a specific foreign-currency payment to know in advance their exact financial commitment in terms of sterling.

Conduct of the import trade

Much that has been written on exporting applies to importing. Thus the foreign seller will need to have information on the British market and on the status of his potential customers here, and the same involved documentation will need to take place. The British bank, of course, will now be acting on behalf of the buyer and will make the necessary arrangements for payment to be made.

Staple commodities are generally sold in the commodity markets referred to above, and because there are agreed standard specifications (with arbitration arrangements to settle disputes) a high proportion of sales can be either by sample or by description. In most cases, intermediaries are used to effect the transactions in the markets.

British firms buying from abroad may use a variety of channels, depending on the same considerations as in the export market. Thus a large manufacturer may import direct, setting up a special department for this purpose; sometimes the foreign firm will set up its own UK branch (as in the car industry); alternatively, import agents working on commission will act on behalf of the foreign seller; finally, in respect of a not inconsiderable proportion of trade, an import merchant trading on his own account will carry out the wholesale function (Chapter 6).

Import controls

In accordance with its international obligation under GATT, IMF and the European community, Britain has progressively removed quantitative restrictions from almost all its imports from countries outside the Soviet Zone and has also substantially relaxed the control of imports from that Zone; there is still a very short list of goods, such as weapons and radio-active materials, which are subject to control and also some restrictions are still imposed on health grounds (e.g. animals, plants and drugs).

Abolition of exchange control

Exchange control was introduced in the UK in 1939 (outbreak of war) to limit the use of currencies to absolutely essential purposes. Gradual relaxation took place after the end of World War II; all controls were abandoned in 1980, since which date permission is not required for the purchase of foreign exchange for any purpose.

Britain and the European Economic Community

On 1 January 1973, Britain, together with the Irish Republic and Denmark, joined the original six member countries – Belgium, France, West Germany, Italy, Luxembourg and the Netherlands – in the European Economic Community (as a result of a referendum, Norway, which had intended to join, withdrew). Subsequently, Greece became a member, and Portugal and Spain are in the queue to join. The enlarged Community forms an enormous trading area of 250 million people and accounts for about a third of world trade. It is intended to offer a basis for the continued economic development of member countries, as well as enabling Europe to play a greater part internationally in political and economic affairs. Membership means, however, that the system of Commonwealth preference (which allowed most of their exports to enter Britain free of duty and about half the British goods exported to the Commonwealth to enjoy lower customs duties than other countries) has had to be largely abandoned, though a transitional period was allowed to help Commonwealth countries to establish other markets. The effect of withdrawing the Commonwealth preference arrangements has led to a considerable decline in the proportion of UK trade with other Commonwealth countries and a substantial increase in trade with other Community countries.

The institutions
The European Economic Community (EEC) consists, in fact, of three communities: coal and steel; economics; and atomic energy. A common market for coal and steel is designed to arrange a regular supply of these commodities to EEC states; funds are raised by a production levy, and investment grants given for modernisation and research and for social measures in connection with staff redeployment.

Community institutions were established in 1957 to formulate and administer the common policies as follows (in each institution Britain has a position equal to that of France, Germany or Italy):

Basic statistics on the ten EEC member states (1979)

	Area (000 sq km)	Population (millions)	Gross Domestic Product (PPS* per head)
Belgium	30.5	9.84	6263
Federal Republic of Germany	248.6	61.31	6993
Denmark	43.1	5.10	6894
France	544.0	53.30	6738
Britain	244.1	55.89	5473
Greece	132.0	9.36	3309
Italy	301.3	56.70	4594
Irish Republic	70.3	3.22	3612
Luxembourg	2.6	0.36	6630
Netherlands	41.2	13.94	6288

*Purchasing Power Standard – a common unit representing an identical volume of goods and services for each country.

(a) *The council of ministers* became the decision-making body, each member directly representing his country.

(b) *The commission* is responsible for policy proposals for submission to the council (Britain has two out of fourteen members, each with a special responsibility for one or more of the main commission activities).

(c) *The court of justice*, whose rulings are binding on member countries, interprets and adjudicates on the meaning of treaties and deals with disputes.

(d) *The European parliament* is now composed of elected members of parliaments of member states (based on political party affiliation) and is a consultative and advisory body. At present 81 out of 434 members are from the UK.

All member countries contribute to a common budget for certain purposes, based on relative total output of goods and services (called *gross national product*), and the contribution of the new members was scaled so that full payments would not be made until 1977 (although later this was delayed).

Common Market policy

By 1977 tariffs on industrial goods had been eliminated between Britain and the Community (after a five-year transitional period) and a common external tariff applied against imports from non-member countries, subject to a few exceptions. Britain has implemented the Common Agricultural Policy, which replaced existing tariff barriers by a system of levies to offset internal price differences and created common price levels within the Community to give producers an adequate return. In this area of agriculture there has been much controversy and food prices in Britain have risen; this country has had to abandon its system of paying subsidies out of taxation to its farmers and, because British agriculture in general terms produces more cheaply than some of the other members, large sums have had to be paid in agricultural support to the Common Market Fund. Special arrangements have been made to give some of the independent developing countries some concessions in trade with Common Market countries, and some preferential trade agreements have been made with a number of other countries known as associate members (e.g. Turkey).

Under the Community regulations, nationals of member countries may freely enter another member state to work there. Restrictions on movement of capital between member countries have been removed. Eventually there will be a standard system of indirect taxes; the first major step was the introduction of VAT in Britain in 1973.

The UK has consistently maintained that the budgetary arrangements for contributions by member countries were unfair, resulting in it being one of the largest net contributors despite its lower income per head than a considerable number of other member states. In particular it has taken the view that the Common Agricultural Policy has too great a share of the budget (almost 70%). Accordingly some adjustments have been made in the contribution arrangements, but the UK is by no means satisfied with these. The problem is a difficult one: though there has been some sympathy for the UK, a number of members (in particular France) have maintained that 'when you apply to join a club you have to accept its rules'.

There was, and still is, very considerable controversy over the question of the advisability of Britain's membership of the Common

Market. The general view of the pro-marketeers, hotly contested, is that Britain's trading position in world markets has been and will continue to be considerably helped by being a member of the world's largest trading group; and that there are considerable advantages from the point of view of world security. Those in opposition to continued membership feel that the financial price already paid (and which payment will continue indefinitely) has been too great; furthermore they express considerable regret at the breaking of Commonwealth links. It is worth noting, in conclusion, that in the first national referendum held in the UK (1975) the country endorsed membership by more than a two-to-one majority.

15

Central and Local Government

In Chapter 1 reference was made to the UK's mixed economy; and public corporations (nationalised industries), which provide services for the consumer mainly in the area of the basic public utilities, have also been dealt with. Some attention now needs to be paid to the way in which the activities of central government and local government authorities affect the life of the business community.

Central government

Parliament is the country's legislative (or law-making) body. But it is the civil service departments that carry out its policies and decisions, in many cases delegating some of these duties to local government and other bodies. Government departments are staffed by permanent civil servants who have no official political affiliations; although in practice an incoming government may bring in a few specialists in an advisory capacity, the civil servants remain to serve their new masters, each department having a permanent secretary, who is the senior officer, and a number of deputy secretaries, each of whom assumes responsibility for an area of work. The minister, as the political head of his department, is responsible to parliament and, as with the permanent secretary, there will be one or two deputy ministers. In some cases, the minister is referred to as 'the secretary of state for . . .'. A number of senior ministers, chosen by the prime minister, form the cabinet or inner policy-making body and non-cabinet ministers will be called in to cabinet meetings when matters affecting their departments are under discussion.

It is not the purpose of this book to deal with the work of government departments in detail; but those interested in business affairs ought to have some knowledge of the work of these departments in business, commerce and industry. Generally it will be appreciated that the main task of the government is to improve the economic position of the country, thus increasing prosperity. This has meant that the policy of successive governments since the 1939–45 war has been to play an increasing role in directing and influencing industry and commerce. Britain is not unique in this situation; virtually all governments accept that this sort of control is essential to a greater or lesser extent. Naturally to carry out this policy large numbers of officials are required in the various government departments. The following outline deals with the main functions of some of the important departments whose work directly impinges on the business life of the community.

The Department of Trade and Industry
Responsibility for general industrial policy is the major task of this department; this includes the sponsorship of private industries, provision of technical services to industry as a whole and carrying out government policy on research and development. Its industrial expansion teams directly assist, both with finance and with advice, firms willing to set up business in the areas for expansion, now called 'assisted areas' (generally those with high unemployment – Scotland, Northern England, Wales, etc.). Another sub-department is the small firms division, whose task it is to assist small businesses to obtain advice and specialist services that they themselves cannot provide. The Department of Trade and Industry is also responsible to parliament for the Post Office Corporation and British Telecommunications (see Chapter 10).

The department also deals with general overseas trade policy, commercial relations and tariffs, including those aspects of relations with the European Community. It is responsible for work in connection with the Companies Acts, supervision of the insurance industry, and has general responsibility for civil aviation, tourism and the newspaper and film industries. Its duties in connection with the encouragement of the export trade through the British Overseas Trade Board and the Export Credits Guarantee Department have already been dealt with in Chapter 14. Consumer protection affairs (see Chapter 16) are largely the responsibility of the Office of Fair Trading in consultation with the Department of Trade and Industry.

Department of the Environment

This 'super' department deals with functions previously the responsibility of three separate ministries – Planning and Local Government, Housing and Transport – and, in fact, there is a minister in charge of each of these fields, with a Secretary of State for the Environment in overall charge.

The department's tasks include assistance and advice to local authorities in house building, the development of New Towns, supervision of water supply and sewerage projects, and a general responsibility for local government finance; in addition, it has a wide range of functions connected with transport. The secretary of state oversees the public corporations in the field of transport (see Chapter 12).

Department of Employment

Like its predecessor (the Ministry of Labour abolished in 1968), this department has a wide range of duties in connection with employment and the use of manpower. These are the collection and publication of information about the demand and supply of labour by industry/region; the operation of the employment exchange service (including special provision for youth and the disabled); supervisory and advisory responsibilities in connection with industrial training and retraining of employees; assistance to both employers and unions to solve industrial disputes; and general responsibility for industrial health, welfare and safety (e.g. factory inspectorate enforcing the Factories and Offices Acts).

Financial and advisory aid to industry

The departments mentioned above, and others, produce a wide range of publications for industry, commerce, employers, workers and consumers. Many of these are the work of the statistics division of the Department of Trade and Industry, e.g. *Economic Trends* and *Trade and Industry*. A visit to the Stationery Office (an example of a business run directly by a government department) will show further examples. In Chapter 14 reference was made to the activities of other government-sponsored bodies which, in addition to the ECGD, assist exporters.

In the field of finance direct help has been given by successive governments to areas and industries with special needs and difficulties. Aid to the 'assisted areas' has been referred to above, and examples of aid to industries can be seen in the considerable financial support given for manufacturing activities sponsored by the Department of Trade and Industry (aerospace, motor vehicles, shipbuilding and steel). Total direct financial aid by the department to all its schemes amount currently to over £1000 million annually. Generous depreciation allowances (see Chapter 11) are given by the Inland Revenue to encourage capital expenditure on plant, machinery and industrial buildings. Financial assistance from EEC funds (see Chapter 14) is also made available in certain circumstances to industries in specific areas.

Mention must also be made of the National Research Development Corporation, an independent public corporation supported by loans through the Department of Industry, which has lent some hundreds of millions of pounds to private industry for research and development projects and to assist in vital production where necessary, often in operations where private funds would not be available. Through its ownership of patents and its joint ventures with industrial companies in development projects, the NRDC has operated profitably for many years. It is anticipated that the NRDC will merge with the National Enterprise Board, a public corporation set up in 1975. Its role nowadays is to make investments, preferably in conjunction with private share investment, in companies exploiting or developing advanced technologies; also to firms in the 'assisted areas', as well as to small firms. Furthermore it is required to sell its shareholdings to private ownership as soon as commercially viable – this has already been done quite extensively. Since 1980 publicly-owned shares held by NEB have been sold for over £120 million (the two largest individual sales being ICL, the computer firm, and Ferranti – both having been successfully saved from financial disaster by NEB investment).

Local government

The two essential characteristics of British local authorities are (i) that they are *local*, each covering an area that is only a small part of the whole country, and (ii) that they are *elected*, each council being controlled by councillors elected by the local citizens. As with government departments, there is a body of full-time paid staff who are responsible for carrying out the policy of the local authority. The council is divided into committees, each running a part of the authority's work: thus there will be a finance committee to control income and expenditure (a local version of the Treasury); an education committee (if the council is an education authority); a public health committee and so forth, depending on the services provided.

Major reorganisation has taken place in local government and since 1974, outside the Greater London area, there have been (*a*) 6 metropolitan counties divided into 36 metropolitan districts and (*b*) 47 non-metropolitan counties divided into over 300 county districts. Examples of metropolitan counties are Greater Manchester and West Midlands – basically heavy populated industrial areas; two typical non-metropolitan counties are Lincolnshire and Leicestershire. The total number of units has been reduced considerably, and the system whereby the towns are administratively separate from the counties in which they lie has been abandoned. All local government functions are divided amongst the four categories. In general terms, those services of a local nature (e.g. refuse collection, housing, local planning) are provided by the district councils and those that need to be organised over a wider area (e.g. police, fire, the wider aspects of planning) are conducted by the county councils. Education is controlled by the non-metropolitan counties and the metropolitan districts. London has a special form of local government: there is the Greater London Council and thirty-two London boroughs plus a special one, the City of London, which has a privileged position because of its centuries of existence.

Status and power

Local authorities can do only what the law allows them to do; their powers are specifically delegated by act of parliament. Government departments exercise general supervision over their affairs and in some areas have direct powers of control; for example, certain major planning decisions require the approval of the Department of the Environment.

Until fairly recently government grants (amounting to around 60%) were paid to local authorities; most local authority borrowing for capital projects had to have (and continues to need) government approval. The 1979 Conservative government, in an attempt to curb the activities of so-called 'high spending' local authorities, introduced financial penalties which, in the case of some urban areas (e.g. London), largely eliminated their grants.

Local authority functions are of two sorts:

1 *Mandatory* – the council *must* carry them out (e.g. education, housing, etc.).
2 *Permissive* – the authority *may* carry them out if it so wishes (example are in the field of entertainment, family-planning clinics, museums and art galleries).

Some authorities provide trading services (already referred to in Chapter 4), where those using the facility pay a direct charge; examples are bus services, docks and harbours, airports, theatres and restaurants. In a few cases, these powers have been granted to them by a special act of parliament.

Local authorities are also responsible for the enforcement of much legislation affecting business, some of which is referred to elsewhere in this book; thus trading standards officers are responsible for ensuring that the provisions of the Trade Descriptions Act are enforced, and similarly for the enforcement of some of the provisions of the Shops Offices and Railways Premises Act, as well as Public Health Acts.

16

Consumer Protection

Reference was made in Chapter 7 to the legal contract that is made every time a sale of goods or services takes place. Both parties to the contract acquire rights and accept obligations. The nineteenth-century attitude of the courts towards contracts for the sale of goods was to let the parties make their own arrangements with the minimum amount of interference from the law; this was the common law doctrine of *caveat emptor* (let the buyer beware). Note that common law is not based on the laws passed by parliament but on rules laid down in previous judgments by the courts, called 'precedents'. The doctrine put the onus on the purchaser to ensure that the goods bought were fit for the purpose for which they were intended – if he made a bad bargain, that was his bad luck.

The *caveat emptor* policy may not have been so bad in the days when the majority of shopping was for simple basic commodities in the village market, but it is hardly a reasonable one in a modern industrial society with its complexity of sophisticated products. For example, to test whether electrical apparatus is both safe and efficient may require involved tests by a specialist with expensive equipment, and a durability test may need a further period of prolonged use. In general terms the consumer is not the 'equal' of the businessman – the 'general public' is not an organised body of people possessing corporately all the relevant facts about possible alternatives to the goods in question, about the quality, about prices. The ordinary consumer is at a disadvantage when coming into conflict with business organisations. This 'weakness' is aggravated by the trend towards concentration in business – in many fields of production the choice of suppliers is fairly limited. Many industries are now dominated by just a few firms – examples being cigarettes, chocolate, soaps and detergents, and banking.

Fortunately the state has long recognised the need for the consumer to have some protection against unsatisfactory products and so gradually a comprehensive system of legislation and machinery to protect the consumer's interest has been created. In certain circumstances traders can not only be prosecuted but compensation may also be awarded to the 'injured' buyer without it being necessary for him to bring a separate civil action. The laws protecting the consumer are now many and complicated and some of the important ones are summarised below.

Common law

There are two main branches – *contract* and *tort*. The former has already been dealt with very briefly: basically if one party fails to carry out his part of the bargain the other can sue in the civil courts for breach of contract. In practice, of course, one is hardly likely to want to sue if only small sums of money are involved – this has always been one of the weaknesses of the consumer protection legislation; the remedy theoretically existed but it was often not a practical proposition. As will be seen later this problem is not as serious as it was, because in some cases the appropriate local authority or other designated institution can take action under criminal law to have wrongs remedied. Tort deals with breaches of a legal duty which people may owe, in certain circumstances, to each other. The best example is the tort of *negligence*, which is governed by a failure to take reasonable care when there is such a duty. The majority of cases are not concerned with the consumer, but one example which comes within this area is the instance of a shopper being injured by slipping on a polished floor in a shop. It must be pointed out that negligence may be hard to prove – the mere fact that you have suffered injury or other loss does not automatically entitle you to recover damages.

At common law one is entitled to a reasonable standard of workmanship when 'services' are involved, for example the repair of a television set. Furthermore, unless a price has been agreed in advance, the charge made must be reasonable, taking into account the circumstances (now embodied in statute law – see below).

Statute law

This term embraces law enacted by parliament in acts of parliament (or legislation). Regulations made by ministers of the Crown under statutory authority also possess the force of statute law. Important Acts are as follows.

Sale of Goods Act 1979

This Act repeals and re-enacts the 1893 Act, which was the first major consumer protection act. Basically the Act (which does not apply when goods are sold privately) states that goods should be of 'merchantable quality and *reasonably* fit for the purpose for which they are intended'. Thus a vacuum cleaner which breaks down after a very short life or picks up very little carpet dirt hardly fulfils these conditions. It is important to remember that the consumer's contract is with the seller (who is normally the retailer) and that if goods are faulty it is the latter's responsibility to refund the cash price paid (though in practice immediate replacement is probably acceptable).

A trader cannot include an 'exemption' clause in his conditions of sale with the intention of taking away rights the buyer has under the Act. Thus 'goods not exchanged nor money refunded under any circumstances' has no validity, because this takes away the buyer's right to reject goods not of 'merchantable' quality. It must be borne in mind that in the case of goods which are reduced in price, or secondhand, or classed as 'seconds', the buyer cannot expect top quality. The Act only gives rise to a civil remedy, which means that, as a last resort, one party may have to sue the other for a breach of contract. However, the trading standards or consumer protection departments of local councils (see Chapter 15) – plus the advice centres or citizens' advice bureaux which are available in many areas – can be of considerable help to buyers and are often able to settle complaints. In general the provisions of the Sale of Goods Act do not apply to private sales.

As a result of the passing of the *Supply of Goods and Services Act* (effective from January 1983), the 1979 Act provisions now also apply to a range of contracts not previously regarded as 'sales', for example contracts for works and materials (e.g. a central heating system installed by a builder); or goods that are hired; or goods obtained by barter (e.g. trading a car in part exchange). Even goods obtained against cereal (or similar) coupons are now included!

Further sections of the Act will provide redress if services provided are unsatisfactory. The Act deals with poor service and workmanship, and stipulates that work must be done within a reasonable time (if not fixed in advance) and at a reasonable price (if not previously agreed). This redress has always been available at common law (see above).

Trade Descriptions Act 1968
This Act is probably the most important safeguard for the consumer. It makes it a criminal offence for a trader falsely to describe the goods or services he is selling – this includes size, materials involved, method and place of production and so on. It is also an offence to make a false comparison between the price currently being charged and the price sold at previously. If, for example, ties are advertised as 'pure silk, manufactured in UK, original price £9.50, sale price £8.25' then it is an offence if the ties are not manufactured in the UK from the material stated; furthermore, they must have been on sale at the old price for at least 28 consecutive days in the previous six months (unless the seller clearly states this is not so). The enforcement of this Act (which again does not apply to persons selling privately) is in the hands of trading standards officers of local authorities (already referred to above).

Unfair Contract Terms Act 1977
This Act is largely concerned to restrict the rights of *businesses* to exclude responsibility for loss or damage, particularly liability for negligence. Thus a business cannot limit its liability for causing death or injury through its negligence. Other exclusion clauses are valid only if they are fair and reasonable. So a car park stating that 'no responsibility accepted for damage to your vehicle on these premises even if caused by negligence of our staff' could hardly rely on this clause to avoid liability.

Food and Drugs Act 1955

This important piece of legislation covers many points. It makes it an offence to sell food or drink which is unfit for human consumption; it controls the manner in which food and drugs are labelled and advertised and lays down standards of composition (e.g. the minimum percentage of meat in a sausage) and controls processing and permitted additives; finally the Act makes hygiene regulations for any premises where food is prepared or consumed, as well as rules about the conduct of employees (e.g. smoking is not allowed by staff handling food). Enforcement is in the hands of local Environmental Health Departments.

Weights and Measures Act 1963

This makes it a criminal offence to sell less than the amount claimed and compels suppliers of prepared foods and some other goods to state the weight or volume of the items concerned.

Consumer Credit Act 1974

Since 1936 there has been some protection for the customer when goods have been purchased on an instalment payment system. This Act strengthens these safeguards and extends their scope to cover most forms of credit. Basically the cash price must always be advised so that the additional credit charge can be clearly seen; the true rate of interest called the Annual Percentage Rate (APR) must be stated. If goods are being obtained on Hire Purchase, although the hirer does not own them till all payments have been made, nevertheless, once a third of the total price has been paid, the goods can only be recovered by means of a County Court order, and in practice it is quite possible that the Court may allow arrears to be paid off gradually. The above regulations apply to most transactions up to £5000. The Act also compels any business connected with the giving of credit to be licensed by the Office of Fair Trading (see next paragraph). Other provisions of the Act deal with the right of a person rejected for credit to obtain a copy of any report on his credit-worthiness that was supplied to the dealer by a credit reference agency; make it an offence for an individual to approach someone *uninvited* and offer to arrange a loan; make provision for court action if the borrower considers an extortionate rate of credit is being charged.

Fair Trading Act 1973
The Office of Fair Trading was set up under this Act. It is a government agency whose job is to keep watch on trading matters in the UK and to protect the consumer against unfair practices. Some ways in which the director general of fair trading helps the public are:

(*a*) By publishing leaflets and so on to help people to get to know their rights.

(*b*) By encouraging trade organisations to prepare voluntary codes of practice which their members accept.

(*c*) By proposing new laws to plug loopholes in the existing law. One example has been the regulations compelling garages to state clearly the price and grade of petrol (and not just '6p off').

(*d*) By tracking down traders who persistently commit offences or ignore their obligations to customers.

(*e*) By checking on the fitness of traders who provide credit or hire goods to individuals and issuing licences under the Consumer Credit Act 1974 (see above).

Encouraging competition

The director general also has a duty to keep a watch on monopolies, mergers and other restrictive or anti-competitive practices.

Monopolies
Where at least one quarter of the UK market for the supply of particular goods or services appear to be controlled by one company (or company group) the director general can refer the matter to the Monopolies and Mergers Commission. If the latter consider the monopoly is against the public interest the secretary of state for trade (already referred to in Chapter 15) has powers to deal with the situation.

Anti-competitive practices
The director general can investigate the conduct of any business which he considers may restrict or distort competition. Small or medium-sized businesses are in some circumstances exempt from

investigation. This is a highly involved subject, and it is dealt with under the Competition Act of 1980. An example might be a finance house (Chapter 8) influencing the vehicle market by tying leasing facilities to a certain make of car.

Restrictive trade practices

The director general has a duty to refer to the restrictive practices court any agreement between two or more parties which accepts some limitation on their freedom to make their own decisions on business matters. An example would be an arrangement by two firms to fix prices. The court will only approve the practice if it is held to be in the public interest.

Powers of Criminal Courts Act 1973

A section of this Act gives the courts the right to award compensation to anyone who has suffered loss or damage as a result of a criminal act (excluding motoring offences). So far the Act has been used on a number of occasions to compensate consumers for losses incurred as a result of Trades Description Act offences by traders.

Other agencies for consumer protection

Citizens' advice bureaux or consumer advice centres run by local authorities exist in most parts of the country to provide information and advice to the consumer. In addition the independent non-statutory National Consumer Council (government funded) keeps a watching brief on behalf of the consumer. Consultative consumer councils exist to deal with individual complaints by consumers as far as the nationalised industries (see Chapter 4) are concerned. There are also a number of private organisations whose task it is to further consumer interests. The largest is the Consumers' Association, which undertakes regular comparative testing of goods bought on the open market; these test reports are supplied to subscriber members monthly in a bulletin named *Which?*. Other bulletins supplied at regular intervals are *Holiday Which*, *Money Which* and *Motoring Which*. Localised consumer protection work (e.g. price surveys in a particular area) is also carried out by local groups whose parent body is the National Federation of Consumer Groups.

Finally, mention must be made of the British Standards Institution (BSI). This is a voluntary, non-profit-making body jointly financed by industry and the government. It prepares and publishes standards in respect of quality, performance, dimensions, testing methods, and so on. Acceptance of these standards reduces unnecessary variety and thus simplifies production. Readers may be familiar with the BS kitemark and standard number on a wide variety of electrical components and accessories (e.g. plugs); motor accessories (e.g. safety belts, crash helmets); and many engineering products. The BSI is governed by a council of representatives of industry, trade unions, professional institutions and government departments.

Commercial Abbreviations

The following abbreviations and terms are commonly used in business and commerce, and are listed here with their meanings.

& and (ampersand)
@ at, for
A1 first class, first rate
a.a.r. against all risks
ab init. *ab initio* (Latin), from the beginning
abt about
a/c, acct account
A/C current account
ad., advt advertisement
ad val. *ad valorem* (Latin), according to value
AGM Annual General Meeting
agt agreement, agent
amt amount
ans. answer
A/P accounts payable
appro. approval, approbation
approx. approximate
A/R accounts receivable
A/S account sales
a.s.a.p. as soon as possible
asst assistant
av., ave average

bal. balance
b/d bring (brought) down
B/D Bank Draft
B/E bill of exchange
b/f bring (brought) forward
bk book

B/L bill of lading
B/P bill payable
B/R bill receivable
Bro., Bros brother, brothers
B/S balance sheet; bill of sale
bx, bxs box, boxes

c cent(s)
C centigrade, celsius
C/A Capital Account
CAP Common Agricultural Policy
carr. pd. carriage paid
carr. fwd carriage forward
cat. catalogue
CBI Confederation of British Industry
cc cubic centimetre; carbon copy
c/d carried down
cf. compare
c/f carried forward
C & F cost and freight
CGT Capital gains tax
chq. cheque
c.i.f. cost, insurance and freight
cm centimetre
C/N credit note
Co. Company
c/o care of
COD cash on delivery

col. column
comm. commission
cont. continued
co-op co-operative
cr. credit, creditor
CS Civil Service
cum. div. with dividend
c.w.o. cash with order

D/A Deposit Account
DB Day Book
D/D Demand Draft
Deb. Debenture
dely, d/y delivery
dept department
dft draft
disc. discount
div. dividends, division
D/N Debit Note
do. ditto (the same)
doz. dozen
D/P documents against payment
dr. debtor, debit
d/s days after sight

ea. each
ECGD Export Credit Guarantees Department
EEC European Economic Community
EFTA European Free Trade Association
enc. enclosure(s)
entd entered
E&OE errors and omissions excepted
esp. especially
Esq. Esquire
est. established; estimated
ETA estimated time of arrival
ETD estimated time of departure
et seq. *et sequentia* (Latin), and the following
ex. without
exch. exchange
ex div., x. div. without dividends

ex int. not including interest
exors executors
exp. express
exs expenses

f, fr. franc(s)
F, Fahr. Fahrenheit
f.a.a. free of all average (used in marine insurance)
FAO for the attention of
f.a.q. free alongside quay; fair average quality
f.a.s. free alongside ship
fcp, fcap foolscap
f.d. free docks
f.i.f.o. first in, first out
FO Firm Order
f.o.b. free on board
f.o.r. free on rail
fp. fully paid
fr. from
frt freight
ft foot, feet
fwd forward

g gram(me)
GA general average (insurance)
GDP Gross domestic product
gen. general
GM General Manager
GMT Greenwich Mean Time
GNP Gross national product
Gov. Governor
Govt Government
gr. grain, grammar
gr. wt. gross weight

HMSO Her Majesty's Stationery Office
HO Head Office
Hon. Honorary, Honourable
HP hire purchase
HQ headquarters
hr, hrs hour(s)

i/c in charge
I/F insufficient funds

IMF International Monetary Fund
Inc. incorporated
ins. insurance
inst. instant, current month
int. interest
inv. invoice
IOU I owe you

J/A Joint Account
JP Justice of the Peace
Jun., Jr Junior

kg, kilo kilogram(me)
kl kilolitre(s)
km kilometre(s)
kw kilowatts

£ pound sterling
l, lit. litre(s)
lat. latitude
lb pound (weight)
L/C Letter of Credit
Led. Ledger
LGA Local Government Authority; Local Government Area
l.i.f.o. last in, first out
long. longitude
Ltd limited

m metre(s), minutes, million
max. maximum
MC Master of Ceremonies
m/d months after date
med. medium
mem., memo. memorandum
Messrs Messieurs (French), Gentlemen
mfg manufacturing
mfr manufacturer
mg. milligram
mgr manager
min. minimum, minute
MIP Marine Insurance Policy
ml millimetre(s)
MP Member of Parliament

m.p.h. miles per hour
m/s months after sight, metre per second

n.a. not available
N/A no advice, not acceptable (banking), not applicable
NB *nota bene* (Latin), mark well, note well
nem. con. *nemine contradicente* (Latin), no one contradicting
N/F no funds (banking)
nil *nihil* (Latin), nothing
N/m no mark
N/O no orders (trading)
nom. nominal
NP Notary Public
NPV no par value
nr near

% per cent
%0 per thousand
o/a on account of
o/c over charge; out of charge
o/d on demand
O/D overdraft, overdrawn
OK all correct
O&M Organisation and Methods
OPEC Organisation of Petroleum Exporting Countries
opp. opposed, opposite
OR owner's risk
ord. ordinary
o/s out of stock, outstanding

p.a. *per annum* (Latin), yearly
PAYE Pay As You Earn (taxation)
p.c. per cent, post card
p/c price current
p.c.b. petty cash book
pcl parcel
pcs pieces
pd paid
per by
per capita by the head

per pro, pp *per procurationem* (Latin), on behalf of
pkg. package
P & L Profit and Loss
Plc Public Limited Company
p/n promissory note
P.O. postal order, post office
pp. parcel post
p. & p. postage and packing
pr, pr. pair, price
pref. preference, preferred
prima facie at first sight
PRO Public relations officer
pro forma as a matter of form
pro tem. *pro tempore* (Latin), for the time being
PS postscript
PSBR Public Sector Borrowing Requirement
PTO please turn over
PV per value

qu. query, question
quan. quantity
qr quarter

R/D refer to drawer (banking)
re. with reference to, concerning
rec(t) receipt
recd received
ref. reference
reg., regd registered
rep. report, representative
retd returned
rly railway
rm ream
R/p reply paid
RSVP *Repondez, s'il vous plait* (French), please reply

$ dollar (money)
SAYE Save As You Earn
sch. school, schedule
SDB sales day book
sec. second

sgn sign(ed)
S/N shipping note
soc. society
spec. specification, speculation
sq. square
SS steamship
St. Saint, street, station
std standard
STD Subscriber Trunk Dialling
stet let it stand
stg sterling (money)
stk stock

TMO telegraph money order
TO, t/o turnover
Tr. Trustee
TT telegraphic transfer
TUC Trades Union Congress

ult. *ultimo* (Latin), last month; ultimatum
UN United Nations
u/w underwriter

v., vs versus; against
var. variety
VAT Value-added tax
via by way of, through
viz. *videlicet* (Latin), namely
vol. volume

W/B Waybill
w.e.f. with effect from
whf wharf
wk(s) week; weeks
w.p.m. words per minute
wt, wgt weight

x.d. ex dividend (without dividend)
x.int. ex interest (without interest)

yr(s) year(s)
yrs yours

Glossary of Commercial Terms

In general, terms defined in the text (see index) are not included here. An asterisk indicates a cross reference.

Air waybill A document made out by the consignor of goods sent by airfreight. It contains full details of the goods (their nature, weight and value), departure and arrival airports, and freight charges.

Annual General Meeting (of a company) The statutory meeting that each registered company is required to hold annually; the major item on the agenda is the approval of the Directors' Report and Accounts.

Asset Anything with a money value (including debtors).

Audit An examination of the accounts of an organisation (often by an independent firm of qualified accountants).

Bankruptcy A situation when the High Court rules that a person is insolvent, i.e. unable to pay his/her debts.

Bear market A situation when prices of stocks/shares on the Stock Exchange are generally falling (see also Bull market).

Bill of Lading A document giving full details of goods being shipped, the name of the vessel and ports of departure and arrival. The holder of the bill is the legal owner of the goods for the time being.

Blue chip A term given to ordinary shares of large and well established public companies (e.g. ICI).

Bonus issue The issue of additional shares to existing shareholders without any payment being required; it will be made in proportion to existing shareholding, e.g. one new share for every three held. From the accounting point of view it is purely a book-keeping double entry, and makes no difference to the net asset value of the company as it is achieved by capitalising of reserves. The Stock Exchange market price will drop proportionately.

Book value   The present book-keeping value of an asset – generally it is the original cost less total depreciation* to date.

Bull market   A situation when prices of stocks/shares on the Stock Exchange are generally rising (see also Bear market).

Capital taxes   Taxes on capital transactions, e.g. capital gains tax, capital transfer tax, land development.

Carriage forward   When a seller quotes a price 'carriage forward' it means that delivery charges from his factory to the buyer's premises are to be paid by the buyer.

Collateral   The security for a loan that may be demanded by the lender (examples are property deeds, share certificates of public companies, and life assurance policies with a 'surrender value').

Conglomerate merger   see Diversification.

Convertible loan stock   A loan stock carrying a fixed interest but with the right to convert at a set date at a set price into ordinary shares.

Corporation Tax   Tax on a company's profits.

Cost, Insurance and Freight   The term used when goods are being shipped or airfreighted from one country to another. It indicates that the seller will pay all freight and insurance costs up to the port/airport of destination (see also Free on board and Free alongside ship).

Cover note   A written confirmation of the proof of existence on an insurance contract pending issue of policy (common in motor vehicle insurance).

Cum dividend   The share price quoted includes the right to receive the dividend due shortly. Thus a company may declare a dividend on March 1st payable to all shareholders on the register on March 10th (see also Ex-dividend).

Debenture (secured)   A loan made to a company whereby the lender has first legal claim on all or a stated part of what the company owns. Sometimes there is a public issue of debenture stock (generally in £100 units) and these will be traded on the Stock Exchange in the normal way. Debenture holders are creditors, not shareholders, and thus their interest is a charge against profits.

Decreasing term assurance   A life assurance with the sum assured reducing each year over a given period; it is very suitable to provide protection for mortgagors (house purchase).

Deed　A formal contract in writing, witnessed and 'under seal' (purely a formality nowadays – sealing wax is not required). Necessary for certain types of contracts (e.g. property sales, deeds of covenant,* etc.).

Deed of covenant　An agreement to make a gift of money regularly for a period of years. Subject to certain conditions this carries financial advantages to the recipient, as he can reclaim the tax that the donor himself had paid.

Depreciation charge　The amount a company takes from its trading profits each year (which sum it retains in the business) to pay for a replacement of its fixed assets (e.g. machinery costs £100000, anticipated life 10 years, annual depreciation charge £10000 so that the whole sum is written off over 10 years). Note that the charge need not be the same each year – under the 'reducing balance' system a much higher amount is charged in the early years. Whatever the method of calculation, the charge reduces profits, thus ensuring that the depreciation charge involved cannot be paid out as dividend (see also Wear and tear).

Direct costs　Costs that vary reasonably proportionately with volume of output: examples are production wages and raw materials. (See also Indirect costs.)

Direct taxes　Taxes paid by an individual or business (based on income) directly to the government: examples are income tax, corporation tax (paid by companies) and capital gains tax.

Diversification　A business in one trade which expands its activities into another and different trade, often in order to spread its risks. (Also referred to as a *conglomerate merger*.)

Dividend cover　The number of times a dividend payment can be met out of the after-tax profits of a company. The more times the profits cover (exceed) the dividend payment, the safer it is that the dividend will continue to be paid even if the company experiences a dip in trade.

Documentary credit　A method of making payments in the overseas trade whereby the importer provides funds through his bank which the exporter can draw upon.

Double tax relief　Bilateral agreements whereby a person earning a part of his income abroad is not taxed twice.

Dow Jones Indices　These indicate the general trend of share price levels on the New York Stock Exchange. Refer to Index numbers.

Drawback　If imported materials which have paid customs duties are re-exported (either as an 'entrepot'* transaction or after processing), the duty paid is reclaimable from H.M. Customs and

Excise. At the time of writing (1983) the experimental use of 'freeports' (an existing example is Hong Kong) is being considered – under these circumstances drawback would become unnecessary.

Entrepot trade Goods from overseas which enter the country purely for transhipment purposes (see also Drawback).

Entrepreneur The decision-maker and risk-taker in a business. The term is used mainly of sole traders and companies where one individual has the controlling interest and actively runs the business.

Errors and Omissions Excepted A term in common use at one time on accounting documents, with the intention of safeguarding the creditor in the event of there being mistakes on the document.

Exchange control Financial regulations imposed at the outbreak of World War II to control the flow of money out of the United Kingdom. After various relaxations they were finally abolished in 1980.

Excise duty The tax levied by H.M. Customs and Excise on a number of items, the main three being alcohol, petrol and tobacco.

Ex dividend The share price quoted excludes the right to the recently announced dividend. The price of the share usually falls by an amount equal to the amount of the net dividend after tax (see also Cum dividend).

Fictitious assets Assets appearing in a balance sheet for technical accounting purposes, e.g. a net loss; they have no realisable 'money' value (compare with Intangible assets).

Finance Act This is the Act of Parliament which makes the provisions announced in the Budget legally enforceable.

Fiscal Used in the terms 'fiscal policy' and 'fiscal year'. The former is concerned with government action to collect taxes and spend them. The latter refers to the tax year which runs from 6 April in one year to 5 April in the following year.

Flag of convenience A technique involving the registration of a ship in another country (e.g. Liberia, Panama) to reduce liability to taxation and to obtain the benefit of less stringent regulations about conditions affecting the crews.

Free alongside ship The seller undertakes to deliver the consignment to the quay at the port of loading. Not as commonly used as Free on board.*

Free on board The seller undertakes to deliver the goods and pay all charges including the loading on to the ship at the port of *departure* (compare with Cost, Insurance and Freight).

Freight   Technically this means the cost of transporting a consignment for a particular journey, though in everyday language it is often used to refer to the goods themselves.

Gearing   If a company has a high level of borrowing or preference shares in relation to its total ordinary share capital, it is said to be highly geared. Low gearing is the reverse situation.

Gilts   see Government securities.

Goodwill   For accounting purposes the net worth of a business is the total of its assets less the total of its liabilities. Particularly when a business is being sold, a goodwill element is added to the purchase price because the buyer is acquiring an existing business – the expectation is 'that the old customers will come back to the old place'. Sometimes this goodwill item is shown indefinitely in the balance sheet as an intangible asset* but more often it is written off over a period of years.

Government broker   The stockbroking firm that acts on behalf of the government when it deals in gifts (see Government securities).

Government securities   Commonly called gilts, because they are considered to be a 'risk free' investment. They bear a fixed interest and, with a few early exceptions, carry a repayment date. Other names they are given are Exchequer Stock, Funding or Redemption Stock. Sometimes a repayment *period* is given, e.g. 13% Exchequer Stock 2003–2005 – the government will choose its own repayment date in this period.

Gross Domestic Product   The total income of residents arising from activities within the UK – effectively it is the gross national product* less any income from abroad.

Gross National Product   The total income of residents arising from activity anywhere.

Hammering   The announcement of the insolvency of a member of the Stock Exchange. Because of the existence of a guarantee fund, members of the public who suffer a loss from the insolvency are normally compensated.

Hansard   The Official Report of Parliamentary Debates, published daily. The records of both the House of Commons and the House of Lords for more than the last 400 years are available in the House of Commons Record Office.

Holding (parent) company   A company that owns more than 50%

of the share capital of another company, called a subsidiary. Often the latter in its turn controls its own subsidiaries.

Horizontal integration   Mergers between businesses producing or distributing the same product or group of products, e.g. two publishers or two supermarket chains joining forces (see also Diversification and Vertical integration).

Implied terms (of a contract)   Terms not specifically stated but which both parties would regard as 'taken for granted' (e.g. that the person offering to sell the goods is entitled to do so).

Imprest system   An accounting system (commonly used for petty cash) whereby a 'float' is established and at regular intervals the cash paid is reimbursed so that the float is restored.

Index numbers   These measure the average percentage change in the prices of a 'set' of items calculated in relation to a 'base' date. For example, the Retail Prices Index measures the retail prices of a group of major consumer goods, the prices being 'weighted' to allow for the relative importance of each item. Roughly speaking, 'weighting' takes into account what the average low-income family spends on the particular item out of every £ of its disposable income. Thus if 5p in every £ is spent on travel and 10p in the £ on heating, then an increase of 20% on the latter will have twice the effect on the Retail Prices Index as the same percentage increase in the former. The 'weighted' price is assumed to be 100 at the base date, then if at a later date the price of the 'set' of items has risen by 10% the new index figure would be given as 110.

There are also volume indices, such as the Index of Industrial Production.

Indirect costs   Production costs that do not change very much (if at all) as production increases. Thus rent, rates and cleaning costs are good examples. (See also Direct costs.)

Indirect taxes   A tax that is not paid direct to the government by the taxpayer but is collected by an intermediary; examples are Value Added Tax and Excise Duty on alcoholic drinks and tobacco products. (See also Direct taxes.)

Intangible assets   Assets for which the value cannot be accurately quantified in money terms, such as goodwill* and patent rights (see also Fictitious assets).

Interim dividend   Many companies pay two dividends yearly; an interim one half way through the year and a final one when the year's financial results are known.

Jobber's turn   A stockjobber quotes two prices – the higher (or offer) price at which he is prepared to sell shares and the lower (or bid) price at which he will buy. The difference is his margin or 'turn'.

Joint and several liability A situation where two or more persons accept responsibility together for the amounts owing and are also individually legally liable for the whole sum. The best example is the general partners in a business partnership.

Joint stock bank A bank that is a public limited company (Plc).

Joint stock company The original name for the type of business that is now known as a limited company; it is still used to some extent.

Kaffirs A Stock Exchange term for South African gold mining shares.

Kruggerand A pure gold coin (which is not currency) produced in South Africa and which (unlike gold bullion) can be purchased by the UK general public.

Legal tender The form of payment which a creditor *must* accept (note that cheques, postal orders, etc., are not legal tender but are called 'representative money'; in practice they are normally acceptable under certain conditions). Bank of England notes are acceptable up to any sum but there are maxima for the various denominations of coin.

Letters of administration A High Court authority to deal with the property of a dead person who has not left a will or who has not nominated an executor in the will. In the former case the rules of intestacy, which set out a priority list of claimants according to the nearness of family relationship, must be followed.

Liquid assets Those assets (including cash itself) with a fixed money value which can 'as of right' be easily and quickly converted into cash. Bank current and deposit accounts are the common ones; stock would not be included because there is no guarantee that a quick sale would be possible. There are degrees of liquidity, according to the speed with which the cash value can be realised.

Liquidation The winding-up of a business, either because the members so choose to do so because it cannot meet its financial obligations (see also Receiver).

Loss leader The practice of selling goods or services below cost to attract customers in the hope that they will purchase other items. It was a common method in the retail food trade but is now illegal. There is no objection, of course, to placing goods on sale at reduced profit margins.

Margin This has two meanings: (*a*) profit margin – see Mark-up; (*b*) dealing on the margin – a Stock Exchange term meaning dealing in shares on borrowed money.

Marginal costs The additional costs per unit of production involved in increasing output. In many cases these decrease as many indirect costs* have already been covered and will not increase as production increases.

Market capitalisation The value the Stock Exchange places on a company. Assume a company has one million £1 shares in issue and currently they are changing hands at 240p then the market capitalisation is £2 400 000; if its earnings (i.e. after-tax profits) for the year are £400 000, then its Price/Earnings ratio is 6 (2 400 000 divided by 400 000).

Mark-up The gross profit on goods (e.g. cost price £25, selling price £30, mark-up £5 or 20%). Note that if expressed as a percentage of selling price (16⅔%) it is referred to as the *profit margin percentage*.

Mergers Two or more companies combining to form one (see also Diversification, Horizontal integration, Takeover bid, Vertical integration).

Minimum Lending Rate This used to be the interest rate fixed by the Bank of England which greatly influenced all other interest rates. It has now been abandoned.

Naked debenture An unsecured debenture*.

'Names' Members of Lloyds insurance underwriting syndicates who are 'sleeping' partners only; they contribute substantial amounts of capital but do not participate in business operations as they are not insurance professionals. However, they do have unlimited liability (refer to Chapter 2 for an explanation of this term).

National Debt This reflects government expenditure over the years that has been financed by borrowing; currently the UK national debt is around £12 000 per head of population. The amount owing to other countries (the external debt) is a burden on the UK balance of payments both as far as interest and capital repayments are concerned. The amounts owing to residents and institutions (e.g. from the issue of government securities, Treasury bills, National Savings, etc.), though having the effect of materially increasing taxation, do not in the end make the community any poorer as only transfer payments are involved (i.e. moving money from one group of people to another).

National income The money value of all the goods and services produced in any year. It is the same amount as national output because all the factors of production – land, labour (including the entrepreneur*), capital – are paid a reward in the form of rent, salaries and wages, profits and interest; and it is the factors of production which are used in producing goods and services. (See also Gross Domestic Product and Gross National Product.)

Offer for sale   A public issue of shares involving an Issuing House buying the entire issue and then re-selling to the public through the issue of a prospectus. The majority of public issues by public limited companies nowadays are made this way.

Official List   The daily list published by the Stock Exchange giving, amongst other information, the bid and offer prices of all quoted securities (see also Jobber's turn).

Oncosts   see Indirect costs.

Operating costs   see Direct costs.

Parent company   see Holding company.

Patent   A licence from the Patent Office giving the applicant (generally for 16 years) the sole rights to an invention or new process. The Patent Office also deals with registration of trade marks and trade names.

Pay As You Earn   Since 1942 employers have had the statutory duty to collect income tax by deduction from pay from their employees. The employer is advised by the Inspector of Taxes how to calculate these deductions, which have to be sent to the Collector of Taxes at fixed intervals. The employer is purely the collecting agent: he has no power to amend the basis of calculation, which is a matter between the taxpayer and the Inspector. Though deductions are made each time an employee is paid, it is the total earned in the tax year which ends on 5 April that is material.

Payment in kind   The Truck Acts forbid payment of total wages in kind (as occurred last century in some industries). However, many employees do receive fringe benefits which are of course payments in kind. Examples are luncheon vouchers, use of company cars for private purposes and free living accommodation. Generally these give the employee some income tax advantage.

Per capita   Per head, as in per capita income.

Per pro   This indicates that a person is signing correspondence on behalf of his employer or principal. However, it only gives limited authority and the principal will not be bound if the person signing exceeds his authority. Much less use is made of 'per pro' in correspondence nowadays than hitherto.

Plimsoll Line   The load line on the side of a ship that shows it is not overloaded; the Department of Trade administers this and many other Merchant Shipping Acts regulations.

Preferential creditor   One who is entitled to be paid before other creditors (e.g. Debenture holders*).

Preliminary expenses   All the expenses incurred in forming a company, which can be very substantial in the case of a public limited company. They appear initially in the Balance Sheet as an asset but are often written off out of profits (as with Goodwill*).

Price/Earnings Ratio   see Market capitalisation.

Price Index   see Index numbers.

Pro-forma invoice   Strictly speaking, this is not a demand for money but an advice. Two cases where it is used: (*a*) when goods are sent to an agent abroad who hopes to sell them, where invoice indicates the anticipated price the supplier hopes to receive; (*b*) when goods are sent on a 'sale or return' basis – if the goods are retained then the payment becomes due; (*c*) when a payment is requested before goods will be despatched.

Public Sector Borrowing Requirement   The amount that a government has to borrow to cover the excess of the expenditure of the entire public sector over its receipts from various forms of taxation. (Generally the UK has a planned budget deficit necessitating this action.)

Receiver   An accountant appointed to run a company which is in financial trouble. He will also be responsible for winding up the company if it has to go into liquidation*.

Redundancy payments   The compulsory compensation paid by an employer to an employee whose job has disappeared because of reduction of demand or introduction of new technology. Payment is based on salary and length of service and a proportion of the sum is met by the government from the National Insurance Fund.

Refer to drawer   The paying bank may 'mark' a cheque in this way if it is not prepared to pay it. There could well be a technical error (e.g. if the cheque is signed by an unauthorised individual); or if there are insufficient funds to meet the payment, the cheque is said to be dishonoured.

Resale Price Maintenance   Until 1964 the supplier could nominate the price at which the retailer had to sell a product to the final consumer, even though there was no contract between the supplier and the retail customer. Under the Resale Price Act 1964 this practice was made illegal unless the Restrictive Practices Court agreed that the 'price fixing' was in the public interest (and it has done so in very few cases).

Retail Price Index   see Index numbers.

Revenue reserves   The portion of the profits of a company that are retained in the company (ploughed back) so as to provide funds for future operations.

Revolving loans   A service provided by banks, retail stores, etc., whereby the customer is allowed to owe his creditor up to a specified limit without having to ask permission each time he borrows (by issuing a cheque or buying goods). The loan is often tied in with a budget account whereby in return for a fixed monthly payment the customer can have credit up to X times that sum.

'Rights' issue   A company needing more capital may offer existing shareholders the right to purchase more shares, usually at a price below the current market price.

'Spot'   This refers to a currency or commodity price. For example, 'spot' sterling is the price of the £ today.

Stagging   'Stagging' a new share issue means applying for shares in a new share issue of a company (which the applicant thinks will be a popular one and therefore over-subscribed) not with the intention of retaining the shares as an investment but in the hope that it will be possible to sell them at a profit when dealings on the Stock Exchange commence a few days later. 'Stags' apply for more shares than they want because they are anticipating that there will be a 'scaling down' when the allotment takes place.

Stock valuation   Unsold stock is normally valued at cost price (or replacement price if this is less). However, difficulties arise where there are large numbers of different stock items, possibly purchased at different prices from several suppliers, and it may not be practicable to keep each batch separate. Two methods of valuation in use are:

FIFO (First in, first out)   This assumes that the oldest stock is sold first, therefore unsold stock will have come from the newer deliveries. If prices are rising, this method tends to push up the valuation.

LIFO (Last in, first out)   The reverse assumption is made: that the newest stock is sold (or used) first, therefore unsold stock will be deemed to have come from the oldest batches.

Takeover bid   One company offering to buy a controlling interest in another company. They may offer cash to the latter's share-holders, or shares in their company in exchange or a combination of both (see also Mergers).

Tax avoidance   The (legal) arrangement of one's financial affairs so as to minimise tax liability.

Tax evasion   The (illegal) non-payment of tax (e.g. as a result of providing false information on a Tax Return).

Taxable income   The amount remaining after deducting the tax-free allowances from total pay.

Time and Motion Study   see Work study.

Trade association   A voluntary body of firms in the same line of business which seeks to protect its members' interests and keep them informed of any developments likely to affect them (e.g. new legislation).

Trustee status   Certain trust funds can by law only invest in companies with trustee status, i.e. those with over £1 million share capital and which have paid a dividend for at least the last five consecutive years. Building societies' funds normally also have this status.

Variable costs   see Direct costs.

Vertical integration   The taking over of a business which either supplies a company with its industrial needs or buys its products. Examples would be a company operating paper mills gaining control of a newspaper, or a soft drinks manufacturer taking over a business which manufactures cans. In the last few decades not a great deal of vertical integration has taken place. (See also Horizontal integration.)

Wear and tear   The loss in value which an asset (e.g. machinery) suffers as a result of its normal use in business activities (see also Depreciation charge).

White Paper   An official statement of government policy on some important economic or social issue. These are published by HM Stationery Office.

Winding-up (of a company)   see Liquidation, Receiver.

Work study   An analysis to discover working methods that will use labour as economically as possible, thus reducing costs; this involves timing employees on particular tasks and sometimes causes resentment amongst them.

Sources of Information

Pamphlets and other useful material may be obtained from the following:

The Stock Exchange, London EC2. In addition the Public Gallery is open from Mondays to Fridays (10am to 3pm) for visitors and a film is also shown on the operations of the Stock Exchange.

Bank Education Service, 10 Lombard Street, London, EC3.

Post Office Marketing Department, 22 Finsbury Square, London EC2A 1PH.

British Telecommunications Headquarters, 2 Gresham Street, London EC2.

National Girobank, 10 Milk Street, London, EC2V 8JH.

Building Societies Association, 14 Park Street, London W1.

British Insurance Association, Aldermary House, Queen Street, London, EC4.

Lloyd's of London (Insurance), Lime Street, London, EC3.

Office of Fair Trading, Field House, 15–25 Breams Buildings, London, EC4A 1PR. The OFT will supply a list of all Consumer Protection publications (some are free, some bear a small charge).

Britain, an official handbook published annually by HM Stationery Office, describes many features in the life of the country, including the workings of government and other major institutions. It is regarded as an established work of reference and contains much of interest for the student and the general reader. It is rather expensive but it is usually available in main public libraries and large college libraries.

Examination Questions

The author and publishers are grateful for permission to reproduce questions from the examination papers of the following bodies: the Associated Examining Board (AEB/GCE); the University of London Examinations Department (LON/GCE); the Royal Society of Arts (RSA); the Institute of Export (Export).

Chapter 1
1 Set out carefully the principal divisions and sub-divisions of commerce and give an idea of the relative importance of each. (RSA)
2 The United Kingdom has a 'mixed economy'. Explain the meaning of this statement. Do you consider any alternative system to be superior?
3 What is meant by 'commercial activities'? Discuss their importance to the economic life of the country.
4 What are 'direct service' occupations? Why is it that underdeveloped poor countries can only afford to spend proportionately small sums of money on them?
5 'The distribution of goods is just as important as the production of them.' Discuss.

Chapters 2, 3 & 4
1 (a) From which sources does each of these forms of business unit obtain its capital: a sole trader, a public limited liability company, and a publicly owned undertaking?
 (b) How may each deal with (i) its profits; (ii) its losses? (LON/GCE)
2 Which form of business unit would you commonly expect to find

engaged in the production and/or sale of each of the following?
Give a reason for your choice in each instance.

(*a*)   electronic accounting equipment costing from £5000 upwards
(*b*)   dental services in a medium-sized town
(*c*)   sale of newspapers and periodicals with delivery over a fairly
small area
(*d*)   building and decorating services with an annual turnover of
£200 000

3   A public limited company wishes to increase its capital. Discuss
three possible methods of doing this.

4   Describe how a large public limited company might undertake
any three of the following:

(*a*)   Raise an extra £1 million of share capital.
(*b*)   Take over a smaller business.
(*c*)   Borrow an extra £1 million for working capital.
(*d*)   Replace its managing director.
(*e*)   Deal with the profit for the year just ended. (RSA)

5   Distinguish between a public company and a private company.
The shareholders in a certain private company have decided to turn
it into a public one. Outline some of the possible reasons behind
such a decision. (AEB/GCE)

6   What influences affect the value of securities dealt with on the
Stock Exchange? (Export)

7   Discuss the advantages and disadvantages of the public joint
stock company as a type of business organisation. (Export)

8   Assess the importance of the services rendered by the Stock
Exchange to the investor, the general public and the government.
(Export)

9   Although the majority of our goods and services are provided
through private enterprise, a substantial proportion are provided
through state-controlled institutions. Explain why this is so.

10   How can I purchase the ordinary shares of a public company?
What risks am I taking in buying these shares? What rights do I
possess as a shareholder? If a company does not pay a dividend, due
to poor financial results, is there any way I can get my money back?

11   Name four industries controlled by public corporations. State
the arguments for and against nationalisation.

Chapter 5

1   Independent shops, multiple shops, department stores and
supermarkets may all be found in most important shopping areas.
Describe the chief characteristics of each of these types of retail

outlet and explain why they can exist side by side in these shopping areas. (LON/GCE)

2 Discuss the changes in shopping habits that have been brought about by self-service. What limitations are there to the extension of the self-service principle? Give your reasons. (LON/GCE)

3 Describe the ways in which a retail co-operative society differs from a multiple store organisation. (RSA)

4 What factors have brought about the great changes in the pattern of retail trade in recent years? (Export)

5 How would you account for the large number of retail concerns in the UK? Do you think their number could be reduced without inconvenience to customers?

6 Briefly state what is meant by 'mail order'. Why is the claim sometimes made that it is a cheaper method of selling than through shops? Why is this not necessarily true? (AEB/GCE)

7 Distinguish between the large multiple and the independent business in retailing. Account for the rapidly increasing percentage share of the retail trade being taken by large multiples at the expense of the independents. How has this affected the wholesale trade? (AEB/GCE)

Chapter 6

1 Give an account of the wholesaler's functions. In what ways is the wholesaler's importance being diminished and how are these functions being taken over? (LON/GCE)

2 (*a*) Give an account of the wholesaler's services to the manufacturer and to the retailer.

  (*b*) How does the public benefit, if at all, from these services? (LON/GCE)

3 Direct selling by manufacturers to consumers is increasing. Explain why this is so, illustrating your answer with examples.

4 'The wholesaler is a useful though not indispensable link in the chain of production.' Explain fully the meaning of this statement, stating whether you agree or disagree with the view expressed.

5 'Middlemen are performing a useful function which helps everybody'; 'middlemen are more likely to help themselves than help the public'. Discuss these contrasting views of the activities of middlemen.

6 (*a*) What is a hypermarket?

  (*b*) What effects is the development of hypermarkets having on (i) the wholesale trade; (ii) unit shops and small multiples? Give reasons for your answer. (AEB/GCE)

Chapter 7

1   (*a*)   What is the importance of cash discount and trade discount to the retailer and wholesaler?

    (*b*)   On June 1 Albert sells goods to John at £720 less 25% trade discount;

        On June 12 John returns one half of the goods;

        On June 14 Albert sells further goods to John at £900 less 30% trade discount;

        On June 30 John pays the amount owing less 5% cash discount.

        How much does John pay Albert?

2   Show how the VAT system of taxation illustrates the true meaning of the word 'production'. Give an example starting from the manufacturing cost of £100 and allow for 15% VAT, to bring out this true meaning clearly. (RSA)

3   List not more than five documents used in connection with purchases and sales on credit (home trade), describing clearly the purpose of each document. (RSA)

Chapter 8

1   Explain the functions of the Bank of England as (*a*) the Government's bank, (*b*) a banker's bank, and (*c*) an ordinary commercial bank. (LON/GCE)

2   What is (*a*) the discount market; (*b*) an accepting house? Describe their functions.

3   In what ways are the joint stock banks (*a*) connected with the central bank; (*b*) controlled by the central bank? (LON/GCE)

4   Why is the Bank of England of such importance in the British monetary system?

5   (*a*)   Write a paragraph on the 'impracticability of barter';

    (*b*)   Describe the desirable characteristics of a good money material.

Chapter 9

1   What is meant by 'legal tender'? With suitable examples explain why, in practice, businesses may prefer to receive debt payments in other ways. What dangers are there in accepting forms of payment other than legal tender? (LON/GCE)

2   Describe the services of the commercial banks which are of especial value to the business world.

3   Describe the various means by which payments can be made through the commercial banks.

4 What is a bank overdraft? What factors would a bank manager consider before granting an overdraft? (LON/GCE)

5 Describe the work of the bankers' clearing house. Draw a diagram showing how a cheque is cleared.

6 'A bank is an institution that holds an umbrella over the trader while the weather is good but takes it away as soon as it starts to rain.' Discuss this statement with reference to overdrafts. (RSA)

Chapter 10

1 Compare the banking services provided by (i) a commercial bank; (ii) the National Girobank.

2 What are the various facilities offered by British Telecom for the transmission of information by the business world? Indicate roughly the speed of each of the facilities you mention. Where can full details of all the facilities be found? (LON/GCE)

3 Write notes on any four of the following: (i) Telex; (ii) Registered and Recorded Delivery; (iii) Subscriber Trunk Dialling (STD); (iv) Business Reply Service and Freepost; (v) Cash on Delivery (COD); (vi) Datel; (vii) Datapost.

Chapter 11

1 (*a*)   Define carefully (i) gross profit; (ii) net profit; (iii) sales turnover; (iv) rate of stock turnover.

   (*b*)   How can a study of the relationship between his net profit and his capital help a trader to decide whether it is worth continuing in business? (LON/GCE)

2 How does a sole trader's balance sheet differ from a statement of profit and loss? Explain the various entries one might expect to see included in a typical balance sheet. (RSA)

3 What is meant by 'rate of turnover'? Why is it important? Work out the annual rate of turnover from the following information.

Net sales for the year	£20 000
Gross profit	£5 000
Cost price of average stock held	£1 500

Are you able to say that this is a fast or a slow turnover rate? (RSA)

4 The following information was extracted from a firm's books for the year to 31 December 19—.

Opening stock: £2 500; Closing stock: £3 000; Purchases: £21 000; Sales: £30 000; Expenses: £6 000.

Find (i) cost of goods sold; (ii) gross profit; (iii) net profit; (iv) gross profit as a percentage of turnover.

Chapter 12
1   In what ways are railways trying to meet the competition of the roads? To what extent have they already succeeded, and are likely to succeed in the future? Give your reasons.
2   Discuss the importance of transport to commerce with particular reference to surface transport within the United Kingdom.
3   (a)   Why have passengers taken to the air so readily, whilst freight is much less easily persuaded into the sky?
   (b)   Describe the effects, current and future, of the large-scale use of containers in transport.
4   What facilities and equipment must be available for the efficient functioning of a modern commercial port? (Export)
5   Discuss the importance of 'containerisation' in road, rail and sea transport. (Export)
6   (a)   What general considerations does a manufacturing firm have to take into account in deciding which type of transport to use when distributing its products?
   (b)   Why might a manufacturer of digital watches use road transport for distribution within the country and use air transport when selling abroad? (AEB/GCE)
7   A business firm which sells its products throughout Britain has, in the past, relied on rail transport for delivery of customers' orders. What would be (a) the advantages and (b) the disadvantages of the firm's changing to a delivery system using its own road vehicles? (AEB/GCE)

Chapter 13
1   Describe briefly the chief risks against which a large manufacturing company might insure. How can an insurance broker help in this connection? Mention one risk against which the company cannot insure. (LON/GCE)
2   (a)   What is the purpose of insurance?
   (b)   How do British insurance companies make a significant contribution (i) to the welfare of individual businesses; and (ii) to the economy of the country? (LON/GCE)
3   Explain what is meant by the statistical basis of insurance and illustrate your answer with a suitable example.
Why are (a) British insurance companies and (b) 'Lloyds' important in world commerce? (LON/GCE)
4   Explain by reference to a fire insurance contract, what is meant by the terms insurable interest, utmost good faith, indemnity and premium.

5   Explain fully the meaning of the statement: 'Insurance is a pooling of risks'.

Suppose a business man has insured his premises against fire for a premium of 2% of their value, and in 20 years he has had no fire and claimed no compensation. What benefits have been received by each party to the contract?

6   A manufacturing company has insured its premises against fire damage. What does it mean if the insurance is extended to cover consequential loss? A fire occurs and completely destroys the premises. When the claim is made, why might the insurance company (*a*) refuse to give any compensation or (*b*) make only partial compensation? (AEB/GCE)

7   Describe the *purpose* of each of the following documents used in insurance: (*a*) proposal form, (*b*) policy, (*c*) renewal notice.

Explain how statistics are important to insurance companies. (AEB/GCE)

8   Describe the insurances which business men may obtain to provide cover for (*a*) damage to or loss of property; (*b*) interruption to a business; (*c*) risks relating to persons. How can an insurance broker assist in the provision of cover? (AEB/GCE)

Chapter 14

1   Discuss the various ways in which overseas debts may be settled. (Export)

2   Describe the problems faced by exporters which arise from differences of language, currency, weights and measures. What other factors create problems for exporters? To what extent have these problems been lessened for British exporters by changes in the United Kingdom? (LON/GCE)

3   What problems face the exporter which do not exist in the home trade? Show how the Government assists exporters to overcome their difficulties. (Export)

4   What are the chief items which make up the 'invisible exports' of the UK at the present time? Why is it so important for the UK to have a favourable balance on 'invisibles'?

5   The United Kingdom (and other countries) often imports raw materials, food and finished goods it is capable of producing itself. Explain why this happens and illustrate your answer with specific examples.

6   Organised commodity markets have existed in the UK for a very long time. What purposes do these markets serve?

Chapter 15

1   Attempt to assess the importance of the work of the (*a*) Department of Trade and (*b*) Department of Industry to the business community.

2   In what ways does the British Government provide direct financial aid to industry?

3   'Local Authorities can only do what the law allows them to do.' Explain this statement, illustrating your answer with examples of services provided by local authorities which impinge on the life of the local business community.

(N.B. Other questions dealing with government activities will be found elsewhere in this section.)

Chapter 16

1   What legislation has been introduced in the post-1970 period to protect consumers against unsatisfactory purchases? Under what circumstances may a customer legally return goods and require the seller to refund the money paid? (RSA)

2   'There is no real need for Consumer Protection. People only have themselves to blame if they do not choose wisely.' Outline a reply to this argument.

3   In addition to government activity in the area of consumer protection a number of voluntary agencies assist the consumer in various ways in the provision of informed advice. Write an account of the work of some of these agencies. Do you think they serve a useful need?

4   Explain what is meant by (*a*) criminal law; (*b*) common law; (*c*) statute law; (*d*) a legal contract. Give illustrative examples where possible.

5   Explain the contribution made by each of the following to consumer protection: (*a*) British Standards Institution; (*b*) Consumers' Association; (*c*) Trade Descriptions Act 1968. (AEB/GCE)

6   (*a*)   What are the advantages of advertising to (i) sellers (ii) consumers?

(*b*)   Outline the protection afforded to consumers against misleading advertisements. (AEB/GCE)

Multiple-Choice Test

In each of the following questions there is only one correct answer. The answers are given on page 224.

1   Mass production is possible only if
   a   the raw materials required are found locally.
   b   consumers will pay a high price for the product.
   c   there is a wide market for the increased production.
   d   many skilled workers live near to the factories.

2   Which one of these statements is *false*?
   a   Commercial services cannot begin until the manufacturing processes have been completed.
   b   If there were no commercial services most goods would not be produced.
   c   Commercial services add values to products.
   d   Every stage of production employs commercial services.

3   The term 'producer' in its true economic meaning refers to one who
   a   grows crops or manufactures goods.
   b   advertises goods or services for sale.
   c   adds value to a product.
   d   provides raw materials or food.

4   A and B are in a formal partnership having contributed capital of £20 000 and £10 000 respectively. Profits will therefore be

    a   divided in a 2:1 ratio.

    b   shared equally, as under the 1890 Partnership Act all partners are equal.

    c   divided according to the amount of business each has obtained.

    d   divided according to the provisions of the Deed of Partnership.

5   Each year every limited company sends to the Registrar of Companies a copy of its

    a   register of shareholders.

    b   memorandum of association.

    c   directors' report and accounts.

    d   sales forecast for the year to come.

6   When the ordinary shares of a limited company have a face value of £1.00 and a market value of 95p

    a   the company has made a trading loss.

    b   the shares are said to be at a premium.

    c   the stockbroker and jobber between them lose the 5p

    d   the capital of the company has not been reduced by the fall in the value of the shares.

7   If a shareholder in a limited company has received no dividends for some years he may well

    a   vote for any resolution proposed at the Annual General Meeting for a change in the Board of Directors.

    b   ask the company to buy back his shares.

    c   appeal to the Department of Trade and Industry.

    d   ask the Registrar of Companies to investigate the company's affairs.

8   One advantage enjoyed by sole traders over limited companies is that

    a   they find it easier to raise more capital.

    b   the personal assets of proprietors are not at risk.

    c   they do not pay VAT.

    d   decisions are more quickly and flexibly made.

9   A limited company made a profit of £100 000 last year. This profit

    a   must be paid to shareholders as dividends.
    b   may be paid to shareholders as dividends if the Board of Directors decide to do so.
    c   must be applied partly to the payment of dividends and partly to the 'ploughing back' of reserves to meet next year's expenses.
    d   must be paid according to the wishes of the ordinary shareholders as expressed in their votes at the Annual General Meeting.

10   Shares in co-operative societies differ from those in public limited companies in that:

    a   shares are quoted on the London Stock Exchange.
    b   there is no maximum shareholding.
    c   shares can be paid for by instalments.

11   If there are too few retail shops, prices may rise because

    a   bigger shops spend more on advertising.
    b   more shop assistants are needed for the bigger shops.
    c   there is too little competition.
    d   customers must buy more goods per customer-visit.

12   A retail co-operative society

    a   passes on its profits to its customers.
    b   has its shares quoted on the Stock Exchange.
    c   passes on its profits to its employees.
    d   must buy all its goods from the CWS.

13   A multiple shop organisation

    a   has many departments in one place.
    b   owns many shops in different parts of the country selling the same goods.
    c   has uniformity of name and style throughout the country.
    d   must be owned by a co-operative organisation.

14   Wholesalers in general

    a   need a considerable amount of working capital.
    b   incur very little risk.
    c   deal only with the manufacturers.
    d   have very high overhead costs.

15   Which one of these statements is *true*?

    a A wholesaler sells cheap goods to the householders on their door steps.

    b A wholesaler is a connecting link between the retailer and manufacturer.

    c A wholesaler only deals in goods which can be sold in very huge quantities.

    d A wholesaler insists on cash payment from his customers.

16   As a retailer I receive a Trade Discount of 20% and a Cash Discount of 5% (one month) from my supplier, so that

    a goods catalogued at £100 will cost me £76 provided I pay within a month.

    b neither discount will be received unless I pay my account promptly.

    c goods catalogued at £100 will cost me £75 provided I pay within a month.

    d both discounts will be shown on the advice note.

17   When I receive a statement of account from a wholesaler this tells me how much

    a is owed to me by my customers.

    b I owe the supplier.

    c money I have in the bank.

    d I have sold in the past month.

18   A UK bank note can legally be

    a refused by a creditor who would prefer a cheque.

    b exchanged for gold at the Bank of England.

    c printed by any UK commercial bank.

    d tendered in payment of a debt.

19   Which one of the following is *not* a function of the Bank of England?

    a Running the bankers' clearing house.

    b Acting as the bankers' bank.

    c Acting as the government's bank.

    d Producing notes and coins.

20 Banks make regular payments on a customer's behalf by means of

    a   standing orders.
    b   cheques.
    c   bankers' draft.
    d   credit cards.

21 A cheque I have paid into my bank is returned to me by my bank marked 'Refer to drawer'. This means that

    a   the cheque was incorrectly drawn, e.g. the date is missing, or the words do not agree with the figures.
    b   I neglected to endorse it before paying it in.
    c   the drawer did not have sufficient money in his account to meet it, and has made no overdraft arrangements with his bank.
    d   the drawer wishes to see me before the debt is settled.

22 Which one of the following best defines a cheque?

    a   An order by a drawer requiring a banker to pay the payee.
    b   A promise by a banker to pay the payee.
    c   A promise by a drawer to pay the drawee.
    d   An order by a bank requiring another bank to pay the payee.

23 I receive an open cheque in payment of a debt. I draw two parallel lines across its face, write my name on the back, and then send it to another person to whom I owe money. In doing so, I

    a   have acted correctly, since my creditor can pay it into his account.
    b   have acted wrongly, since I had no right to cross the cheque.
    c   need not have endorsed it.
    d   have prevented my creditor from passing it on again to his creditor.

24 Your organisation wishes to make an urgent delivery of
samples from London to Glasgow. Which of the following
services would be the most suitable?

    a Freepost.
    b Datapost.
    c Datel.
    d Recorded Delivery Service.

25 A business wishes to circularise potential customers about a
'special offer' involving filling up a form and returning it. The
facility most useful for this purpose is

    a an advertisement (with coupon) in books of stamps.
    b the Business Reply Service or Freepost.
    c Datel.
    d cash on delivery.

26 Given that a trading company in a given year had:

Opening Stock	£400	Closing Stock	£600
Purchases	£5200	Sales	£10000

its rate of stock turnover for the year is

    a 100%
    b 200%
    c 10 times
    d 20 times

27 Most trading businesses in UK aim to have

    a low expense rate, short period of credit allowed, low rate
of stock turnover and negligible working capital.
    b low expense rate, high rate of stock turnover, short
period of credit allowed and adequate working capital.
    c short period of credit allowed, high working capital, high
gearing of capital and low rate of stock turnover.
    d high working capital, long period of credit allowed, low
rate of stock turnover and high capital gearing.

28 An average stock of £20 000 (at cost) being turned 10 times a year at a gross profit rate of 20% on sales, with expenses of 10% on turnover, would show a net profit of

   a £16 000
   b £26 000
   c £25 000
   d £20 000

29 'Tramp' vessels are those ships that provide a

   a coastal service only.
   b service that is at owner's risk, i.e. no marine insurance company will undertake to insure the cargo being carried.
   c regular, scheduled service between ports, i.e. to a published timetable.
   d service that can be chartered.

30 Containerisation involves the

   a standard sizing of transport units.
   b preparation of goods for deep freeze storage.
   c attractive packaging of goods.
   d selling of pre-packed goods in supermarkets.

31 If an insurance company calculates that there is one chance in ten that a certain event will occur in the course of a year, it will

   a charge a premium of rather more than 10% of the value of the goods insured.
   b pay out not more than nine-tenths of the value of the goods in any claim.
   c give back one-tenth of the value of the goods if the event does not occur this year.
   d refuse to pay out on more than one claim per ten years.

32 A trader insures his plate-glass windows against damage. If he receives £100 from the insurer to make good some damage, this payment is

   a indemnity.
   b insurable interest.
   c premium.
   d capital gains.

33 Those who accept risks at Lloyd's are known as

  a actuaries.
  b agents.
  c underwriters.
  d jobbers.

34 A basic principle of insurance is that the insured must not fail to disclose any material fact. This principle is known as

  a utmost good faith.
  b insurable interest.
  c proximate cause.
  d indemnity.

35 An invisible import is

  a purchase of goods and services by Americans on holiday/business in the UK.
  b natural gas.
  c purchase of goods and services by UK citizens on holiday/business in America.
  d illegal immigrants.

36 Entrepot trade relates to goods

  a entering the country illegally.
  b to be re-exported.
  c to be processed.
  d on which tax has to be paid.

37 The terms of trade show the

  a relationship between exports and imports by value.
  b change of export prices over time.
  c value of exports in any one year.
  d value of exports minus imports in any one year.

38 If Britain devalues her currency against the US dollar

1 my holiday in the United States will cost me more.
2 the price of British cars in American showrooms will go up.
3 American imported goods will cost more in British shops.
4 the British Terms of Trade with the United States will become unfavourable.

a All of these are true
b Only *1*, *2* and *3* are true
c Only *1*, *3* and *4* are true
d Only *3* and *4* are true

39 This table shows a country's balance of payments for 1984

Exports	£250 million
Imports	£280 million
Invisible Surplus	£20 million
Capital Account Surplus	£25 million

Which one of the following is *false*?

a The country has a visible deficit for 1984.
b The country has a current account surplus for 1984.
c The country has a balance of payments surplus for 1984.
d The country has a balance of trade surplus for 1984.

40 In which one of the following methods of obtaining goods on credit does ownership of the goods *not* pass immediately to the purchaser?

a Credit sale
b Hire purchase
c Budget account
d Bank credit card

Answers to Multiple-Choice Test

1	*c*	**11**	*c*	**21**	*c*	**31**	*a*
2	*b*	**12**	*a*	**22**	*a*	**32**	*a*
3	*c*	**13**	*b*	**23**	*a*	**33**	*c*
4	*d*	**14**	*a*	**24**	*b*	**34**	*a*
5	*c*	**15**	*b*	**25**	*b*	**35**	*c*
6	*d*	**16**	*a*	**26**	*d*	**36**	*b*
7	*a*	**17**	*b*	**27**	*b*	**37**	*a*
8	*d*	**18**	*d*	**28**	*c*	**38**	*b*
9	*d*	**19**	*d*	**29**	*d*	**39**	*d*
10	*b*	**20**	*a*	**30**	*a*	**40**	*b*

Index

Please also refer to *Commercial Abbreviations* (page 190) and *Glossary of Commercial Terms* (page 194)

accepting houses, 86, 170
accident insurance, 144, 145, 151, 152–3
accounting principles, 17, 116–27
air transport, 36, 137–8
Annual Percentage Rate, (APR), 186
annuities, 155
Articles of Association, 18, 19, 44
assets, 31, 38, 116–21
assisted areas, 177, 179
Atomic Energy Authority, 36
aviation insurance, 153–4

bad debts, 127, 153
balance of payments, 162, 163–7
balance of trade, 163–7
balance sheets, 31, 116–21
Baltic Exchange, 170
bankers' clearing house, 95, 98
banker's draft, 94
bank giro, 97–9
Bank of England, 5, 36, 81, 83–5, 95, 97
banks, 9–10, 80–6, 87–105, 108
  loans, 99–102, 104
  overseas, 158, 163, 168–9
barter, 80, 82, 185
Beeching Report, 134
bills
  of exchange, 76, 82–3, 85, 86, 89, 169
  of lading, 169
Bretton Woods Agreement, 161, 162
British Airports Authority, 137
British Airways, 39, 138
British Broadcasting Corporation (BBC), 35
British Insurance Association, 148
British Overseas Trade Board (BOTB), 167–8, 169, 177
British Railways Board, 133–4
British Standards Institution (BSI), 188–9
British Telecommunications (BT), 39, 40, 106, 112–15, 178, 206
British Transport Commission (BTC), 132–3
British Transport Docks Board, 133–4
Bureaufax, 115
business
  reply service, 110
  transactions on credit, 67–77

canal transport, 129–30
capital, 11, 26–7, 116–22, 174
cash, 76, 80–3
  dispensers, 90

cash – *cont.*
  with order (CWO), 75
caveat emptor, 146, 182
central government, 3–5, 176–9
Central Trustee Savings Bank, 95
Certificate of Incorporation, 18
Certificate of Trading, 18
chambers of commerce, 169
cheque cards, 94, 107, 108
cheques, 76, 81, 82–3, 88–95, 98
circulating capital, 120
citizens' advice bureaux, 188
Civil Aviation Authority, 137
clearing
  banks, 95
  house system, 88, 95–7, 98
commercial service occupations,
  8–9
commodity markets, 62, 164, 170,
  171
Common Agricultural Policy,
  167, 174
common law, 183–4
Common Market *see* European
  Economic Community
Common Market Fund, 174
Commonwealth trade, 172
companies
  joint-stock, 15–16, 86
  limited by guarantee, 17–18
  limited by shares, 16–17
  main features, 18–21
  private limited, 16, 21, 42–3
  public limited, 16, 21, 42–3
  unlimited, 17
Companies Acts
  1844, 16
  1855, 16
  1967, 17
  1980, 16, 18, 21
  1981, 12, 17, 18–19, 21
Competition Act 1980, 188
Confederation of British
  Industries, 169
consumer advice centres, 188
Consumer Credit Act 1974, 186,
  187

consumer protection, 182–9
Consumers' Association, 188
containerisation, 135–6
contribution (insurance), 147–8
Co-operative Bank, 63, 95
Co-operative Insurance Society,
  44, 63–4
co-operative societies
  business, 40–5
  retail, 53–4
Co-operative Wholesale Society
  (CWS), 44, 63–4
Council of the Stock Exchange,
  18
credit
  cards, 94, 100–1, 104–5, 113
  notes, 73–4
  terms, 69
  transfer system, 76, 83, 97–9
current accounts, 87–95
Customs and Excise Department,
  79

Datapost, 111
Datel, 114
debenture
  interest, 40
  stock, 26
delivery notes, 71–2, 73
deposit accounts, 87, 99
depreciation, 119, 126–7
dictum meum pactum, 29
direct
  debiting, 98–9, 108
  service occupations, 8–9
discount houses, 85, 86, 170
diseconomies of scale, 6
dividends, 20, 27, 31–4, 44, 63
documentary credit, 169
drawings (accounting), 120

economies of scale, 6
employers' liability insurance,
  152
Employment, Department of, 178
Employment Protection Act
  1975, 45

endowment assurance, 155
Environment, Department of, 178, 181
European Communities Act, 19
European Economic Community (EEC), 17, 65, 167, 172–5, 177, 179
exchange
  control, 171–2
  equalisation account, 85
expenses, 119, 126
  fixed, 125
  variable, 125
export credit insurance, 168
Export Credits Guarantee Department (ECGD), 153, 168, 170, 177
export trade, 157–70
  invisible, 163–4, 170
  visible, 163–4
extractive occupations, 8

Fair Trading Act 1973, 187
fidelity guarantee insurance, 153
fiduciary issue, 82, 84
finance houses, 86
fire insurance, 144, 148, 151–2, 153, 156
fixed capital, 121
Food and Drugs Act 1955, 186
foreign exchange, 103, 107
Foreign Exchange Market, 170
freefone, 113
freepost, 110
freightliners, 134, 135
Friendly Societies, 148–9
futures trading, 170

Gaming Act 1845, 145
General Agreement on Tariff and Trade (GATT), 162, 171
giro banking, 97–9
government securities, 25–6, 100, 156
gross national product (GNP), 173

high speed trains (HST), 139
Highways Act 1555, 128
hire purchase, 58, 86, 186

import trade, 157–67, 171
  invisible, 163–4
  visible, 163–4
indemnity, 147–8, 153
Independent Broadcasting Authority, 36
Independent Television Authority, 36
Industrial and Provident Societies Acts 1965, 41, 44
Industrial Life (or Home Service) Assurance Companies, 148–9
industry, 5–7, 8
  government aid, 7, 178–9
insurable interest, 145–6
insurance, 9–10, 142–56
  brokers, 150
  main types of, 151–6
Inter-City services, 139
International Civil Aviation Organisation, 141
International Monetary Fund (IMF), 162, 171
invoices, 71, 72, 73–4
issued capital, 20
issuing houses, 30, 31

jobbers, 27–8, 29–30
joint-stock
  banks, 168–9
  companies, 15–18, 86

ledger accounts, 73, 74–5
liabilities, 31, 116–21
life assurance, 144, 146, 147, 148–9, 154–6
Life Assurance Act 1774, 145
Life Offices Association, 148
limited liability companies, 11, 14, 16–21, 39
Limited Partnership Act 1907, 14
Lloyd's of London, 149–50, 154, 206

loan capital, 121–2
loans, 25–6, 99–102, 104, 121–2
local government, 4–5, 35, 178, 180–1, 184, 185
London Commodity Exchange, 170
London Passenger Transport Board, 35, 132
London Transport Board, 133–4

magnetic ink character recognition (MICR), 90, 96
manufacturing occupations, 8–9
marine insurance, 144, 146, 150, 151, 153–4
Marketing Boards, 64–5
Memorandum of Association, 18–19, 39
merchant banks, 86, 97, 168–9
Metal Exchange, 170
Minimum Lending Rate (MLR), 102, 168
mixed economies, 4–5
monopolies, 3, 5, 6, 38, 187
Monopolies and Mergers Commission, 187
motor vehicle insurance, 145–6, 147, 150, 152–3

National and Local Government Officers Association (NALGO), 45
National Bus Company, 40, 139, 141
National Consumer Council, 188
National Economic Development Council (NEDC), 45
National Enterprise Board (NEB), 179
National Federation of Consumer Groups, 188
National Freight Company, 38, 140
National Freight Corporation, 38
National Girobank, 76, 95, 106, 107–8, 206
National Research Development Corporation (NRDC), 179
nationalised industries, 4–6, 35–40, 188
nominal capital, 20
North Sea Oil, 164

Office of Fair Trading, 177, 186–7
ordering, 69–72
overdrafts, 100, 101–2
overseas
  insurance, 151, 158, 163
  trade, 29, 103, 157–75
    financing, 169–70
    government aid, 167–8, 177
    non-government aid, 168–9

Partnership Act 1890, 13
Partnership Agreement, 13
Partnership Survivorship Assurance, 14
partnerships, 11, 12, 13–15, 42–3, 49–50, 121
Passenger Transport Authority (PTA), 139
payment methods, 76–7, 88–90, 97–9, 108, 169–70
pipelines, 138
Port of London Authority, 34
postal orders, 76, 106–7
Post Office, 35, 39, 40, 178
  postal services, 109–11
  remittance services, 76, 106–9
Post Office Users' Council, 40
Powers of Criminal Courts Act 1973, 188
Prestel, 114
principle of comparative costs, 157
private
  automatic branch exchange (PABE), 112–13
  limited companies (Ltd), 16–21, 42–3
  sector, 2–3, 37–8, 41, 42–3
    finance, 25–34
    structure, 11–24

productive occupations, 8–10
profit and loss accounts, 122–7
proforma invoice, 75
proximate cause, 148
public
  corporations, 35–40, 42–3
  liability insurance, 153
  limited companies (Plc),
    16–21, 25, 42–3
  sector, 35–40, 42–3
Purchase Tax, 77, 79
Purchasing Power Standard
  (PPS), 173

quotations, 68–9

rail transport, 4, 36, 129, 130–5,
  139–40, 141
Railway and Canal Traffic Act
  1854, 129
Railway Regulation Act 1844,
  129
re-exports, 163
Registrar
  of Companies, 18
  of Friendly Societies, 44
Registration of Business Names
  Act 1916, 12
registration of companies, 16–17,
  19
re-insurance, 150–1
remittance advice, 76
restrictive trade practices, 188
retailing, 6, 46–59
  automatic vending, 48, 57
  co-operative societies, 53–4
  department stores, 50–1, 53
  discount stores, 56
  hypermarkets, 48, 55
  mail order, 48, 56–7, 76, 110
  multiple stores, 48, 51–2, 53,
    54, 58
  self-service, 48, 51, 54–6
  shopping precincts, 48, 52,
    55–6
  small-scale, 14, 49–50
  supermarkets, 48, 53, 54–6

  superstores, 55
  variety chain stores, 53
Road and Rail Act 1933, 131
Road Fund, 131
Roads Act 1920, 131
Road Traffic Act 1930, 131
road transport, 36, 128, 130,
  131–2, 139–41
Rochdale Society of Equitable
  Pioneers, 41
roll-on roll-off, 136, 137
Royal Charter, 15, 35

Sale of Goods Acts
  1893, 184
  1979, 184–5
Scottish Wholesale Society
  (SCWS), 44
Selectapost, 111
Select Committee of Nationalised
  Industries, 39
Selective Employment Tax, 77
Serpell Report, 141
shares
  co-operative society, 44–5
  issue of, 18, 21, 30–3, 38, 86,
    104
  ordinary, 20–1, 31–4
  preference, 20–1, 26, 31–4
  transfer of, 16–17, 25, 27
shipping, 136–7
sleeping partner, 14
Society for Protection of the
  Average Retailer, 50
sole trader, 11, 12, 42–3, 49–50,
  54, 121
Speedlink, 135
standing orders, 98–9, 108
statements of account, 75–6, 90
Stationery Office, 35
statute law, 184–7
stockbrokers, 27–8
Stock Exchange, 25–34, 102, 103,
  156, 206
Stock Exchange Council, 27
Stock Exchange Daily List, 28, 29
stocks and shares, 25–7, 40

stockturn, 122
subrogation, 147–8
subscriber trunk dialling (STD),
    112–13
Supply of Goods and Services Act
    1983, 184–5

taxation, 5, 14, 35, 103, 174
telegrams, 113–14
telemessages, 113–14
Telex, 114
term assurance, 155
terms
    of sale, 67–79, 182
    of trade, 160–1
trade, 9, 10
    associations, 169
Trade and Industry, Department
    of, 12, 13, 18, 167–8, 177,
    178, 179
Trade Descriptions Act 1968,
    181, 185, 188
trade unions, 37, 45
Trades Union Congress, 45
trading standards officers, 12, 185
Transcash, 107, 108
transport, 9, 10, 128–41, 178
Transport Acts
    1943, 133
    1947, 132, 133
    Disposal of Road Haulage
        Property 1956, 133
    1962, 133

1968, 131, 139
1980, 141
1981, 141
Transport and General Workers
    Union (TGWU), 45
Transport Holding Company,
    133–4
Transport Internationale Routier
    (TIR), 137
Transport Tribunal, 133
Treasury Bills, 85, 101
turnover, 122–3

uberrima fides, 146–7
underwriters, 149–50, 154
Unfair Contract Terms Act 1977,
    185
uninsurable risks, 143
unit load, 135–6
unlimited liability, 12, 13, 14, 16,
    17, 27

Value Added Tax (VAT), 29, 68,
    77–9, 174
vicarious liability, 153, 154

warehousing, 9, 50, 62
Weights and Measures Act 1963,
    186
Whiteley, William, 50
wholesaling, 14, 60–6
working capital, 120
World Bank, 161–2